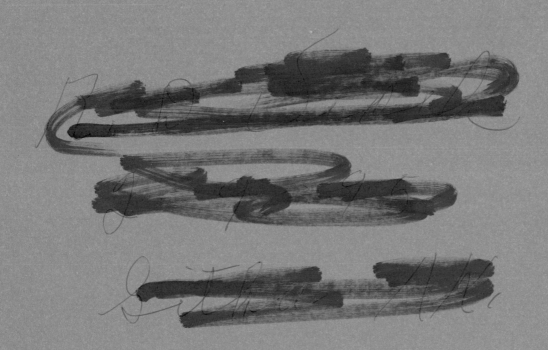

MEMOIRS OF ROBERT E. LEE

MEMOIRS OF ROBERT E. LEE

A. L. LONG

Edited and abridged by Stanley Schindler

Crescent Books
New York

PAGE 1
Robert E. Lee in 1863.

PAGE 2
Lee and Stonewall Jackson.

LEFT: General Armistead L. Long.
BELOW: Lee at the Battle of Spottsylvania, 1864.

CONTENTS

Editor's Preface...6

Introduction...8

The Seven Days' Campaign...16

Second Bull Run...30

Antietam...44

Fredericksburg...62

Chancellorsville...78

Gettysburg...96

Wilderness, Spottsylvania, and Cold Harbor...124

The Siege of Petersburg...142

Appomattox...156

General Lee as a Soldier...170

Index...190

This 1994 edition published by Crescent Books,
distributed by Outlet Book Company, Inc.,
a Random House Company,
40 Engelhard Avenue
Avenel, New Jersey 07001

Produced by
Brompton Books Corporaiton
15 Sherwood Place,
Greenwich, CT 06830

ISBN 0-517-10333-8

8 7 6 5 4 3 2 1

Printed and bound in China

Editor's Preface

Unlike many of his famous contemporaries in both the Confederate and Union armies, Robert E. Lee, greatest of all the Southern commanders, never wrote a personal memoir describing the pivotal role he played in the Civil War. That he fully intended to do so is evident. In June 1870, for example, he wrote a cousin, Cassius Lee: "I have had it in my mind to write [a history] of the campaigns in Virginia, in which I was more particularly engaged. I have already collected some materials for the work, but . . . I have not commenced the narrative."

Nor would he. Less than five months later, on October 12, 1870, "Marse Robert" would die quietly in his home in Lexington, Virginia. It is said that among his last audible words were: "Strike the tent!" and "Tell Hill he *must* come up."

That Lee did not live to complete his memoirs has been a source of keen regret to historians ever since. To be sure, much of his private correspondence and his official dispatches survive, but to catch intimate glimpses of the man himself in

Robert E. Lee is portrayed here as general-in-chief of all the armies of the Confederacy. The generals shown with him include Joseph E. Johnston (at Lee's right in the front row), whom Lee succeeded as commander of the Army of Northern Virginia after Johnston was wounded at the Battle of Seven Pines on May 31, 1862. Ambrose P. Hill, one of Lee's favorites (at the left, heavily bearded, holding his hat at his side), died at Petersburg on April 2, 1865. It was his name that Lee cried out on his deathbed. Stonewall Jackson (at Lee's left in the front row), the man on whom Lee most depended, was lost to him at Chancellorsville in May 1863. The other officers depicted are, from the left, John Bell Hood, Richard Ewell, Braxton Bragg, Albert Sidney Johnston, Wade Hampton, E. Kirby Smith, Jubal Early, [Hill], S. D. Lee, R. H. Anderson, John B. Gordon, T. S. Holmes, W. G. Hardee, [Johnston], Simon Buckner, James Longstreet, Leonidas Polk, [Lee], Nathan B. Forrest, P. G. T. Beauregard, [Jackson], Samuel Cooper, J. E. B. Stuart, Richard Taylor, J. C. Pemberton, and D. H. Hill.

action, posterity has been obliged to rely almost entirely on the reminiscences of his wartime associates. Fortunately, many of these exist, and probably the most authoritative and comprehensive – both because of the nature of the association and because of its long duration – are to be found in *Memoirs of Robert E. Lee* by General Armistead L. Long.

Long, a fellow Virginian and a West Point graduate, had entered Confederate service in 1861 and had soon become Lee's chief of artillery when Lee commanded the Southern Department. In March 1862 Lee was made President Jefferson Davis's military advisor, and Lee at once appointed Long to be his personal military secretary, a post Long would hold until the latter part of 1863. He was thus continuously at Lee's side throughout the Seven Days' Battles, Second Manassas (Second Bull Run), Sharpsburg (Antietam), Fredericksburg, Chancellorsville, and Gettysburg. And even after Lee regretfully returned Long to combat service (as a brigadier general commanding the

artillery of the Army of Northern Virginia's Second Corps), the two men remained in close association for the remainder of the war and, indeed, for the remainder of Lee's life.

This abridged and illustrated edition of Long's *Memoirs* concentrates heavily on the period when Long served directly under Lee. Additional biographical material concerning Lee's life prior to the time he assumed command of the Army of Northern Virginia – material added by Long at his publisher's request – is summarized in the Introduction which follows this Preface. The most illuminating passages of Long's accounts of his time with Lee are presented in full. Bridging passages between these narratives are also in Long's own words but are condensed, ellipses marking the omission of words or sentences and three asterisks between lines denoting the omission of paragraphs. The result, we hope, is a faithful and colorful rendition of a work that has now come to be regarded as one of the classics of Civil War literature.

Introduction

Robert Edward Lee, commander of the Confederate armies in the American Civil War, was called by his contemporary biographer A. L. Long "the man whom future ages will undoubtedly name as the greatest military genius of the nineteenth century." He was worshipped as a hero by his men, and his memory has been cherished through succeeding generations. Inspiring praise and devotion not only for his brilliance and daring in war but for his consideration and humility, Lee was a consummate soldier and a genuinely great man.

He was the product of an illustrious lineage going back to the Norman Conquest of England. The more immediate Southern aristocrats from which he was descended originated with

LEFT: General Robert E. Lee, in a Mathew B. Brady photo taken at Lee's Richmond home one week after the surrender of his army at Appomattox.

OPPOSITE: A genealogical tree, published after Lee's death in 1870, traces the six generations of the Lee family descended from Col. Richard Lee, who emigrated to Virginia in 1641.

ABOVE: Richard Lee, who established the American branch of the Lee family.

BELOW RIGHT: Henry "Light-Horse Harry" Lee, Robert E. Lee's father.

Richard Lee, who came to Virginia in 1641 as colonial secretary under governor Sir William Berkeley. His grandson, Thomas Lee, was the first native-born American to hold the office of royal governor of the colony of Virginia. Thomas left eight children, including Richard Henry, a notable member of the Continental Congress and a signer of the Declaration of Independence; Francis Lightfoot, also a member of the Congress and a signer of the Declaration; and Arthur, a diplomat known in London for his letters to the press signed "Junius Americanus" defending the colonial struggle with England.

Thomas Lee's younger brother Henry sat in the early councils of the Virginia colony. His son, also Henry, sat in the House of Burgesses. The eldest of this Henry's eleven offspring was the American cavalry officer Henry Lee (born in 1756) who won the name "Light-Horse Harry" for his exploits in the Revolution.

Three years after the death of his wife in 1790, Light-Horse Harry Lee, now governor of Virginia, married Anne Hill Carter. The third of five children of this marriage, and the youngest son, Robert Edward, was born in 1807 (according to family tradition in the same room of the Westmoreland County mansion, "Stratford," as were the two Lee's who signed the Declaration).

R. E. Lee's father served in Congress from 1799 to 1801, when he retired to private life and began to indulge a passion for land speculation. A poor businessman, ultimately hounded by creditors who saw him confined for a year in debtors' prison, Light-Horse Harry unsuccessfully sought government appointments abroad. Revenue from his wife's estate could provide food, clothing, and shelter, so the family moved from Stratford – now owned by Robert's half-brother – to a small house in Alexandria, Virginia.

In 1812 Robert's father was seriously injured while helping to defend a young Baltimore newspaper editor from personal assault. In failing health, unable to serve in the second war with England, he left his family and country to find his health in Barbados. Robert, now six years old, never again saw his father; while returning to Virginia in 1818, Light-Horse Harry Lee died at the Georgia home of his old commander, Nathanael Greene.

"Robert was always good, and will be confirmed in his happy turn of mind by his ever-watchful and affectionate mother," his father wrote of him, noting his essential character. Robert's first academic instruction came from his mother, but he was soon sent to the Carter family school; his mother's family was so large and close that it supported a school for the family's girls and another for the boys. By the age of 13 Robert had outgrown the family school and, probably in 1820, enrolled at the Alexandria academy. Completing a typical classical curriculum in 1823, he decided to pursue his hereditary leaning toward a military life and applied for and received an appointment from Secretary of War John C. Calhoun to the U.S. Military Academy at West Point, beginning March 17, 1825.

The self-controlled young man who would later declare that "duty was the most sublime word in the English language" was graduated second in his class of 1829 without a single blemish on his record. His professional interest was engineering, and he was commissioned brevet second lieutenant of engineers and assigned to Fort Pulaski, Georgia.

When Robert came home from West Point he hurried to visit

21-year-old Mary Anne Randolph Custis, the only surviving child of George Washington Parke Custis, who was a grandson of Martha Washington and the adopted son of her husband George. Shortly after Lee's transfer in 1831 to Fort Monroe, Virginia, Mr. Custis reluctantly consented to a marriage of his daughter to this soldier with poor financial prospects and the likelihood of being much absent from home. Mary would bear Lee seven children in fourteen years; their three sons would serve in the Confederate army, two as generals.

In August, Lee and Mary arrived at Fort Monroe, where they would reside for three years. Though ill part of the time and often at Arlington, her parents' home, Mrs. Lee had their first child in September 1832. In these years Lee became fully qualified at directing large engineering projects, and in 1834 he was assigned to Washington, D.C., as assistant to the chief of engineers. His family was happily established at Arlington, while Lee usually rode on horseback to his office each day in the capital.

For a year Lee attended to office duties, which he found dull, though the social life of Washington appealed to him. In 1835 a boundary dispute between Ohio and Michigan territory required his service for the summer with a survey team. He embarked on no other outside assignments until 1837, when he found the opportunity to volunteer for engineering projects to improve St. Louis harbor and ship channels on the Mississippi. Much of this was pioneering work which won him praise, and he was commissioned captain in August 1838.

When federal money for the projects was terminated, Lee returned to Washington in 1840 as a military engineer of recognized reputation. A year later he was able to select an assign-

ABOVE LEFT: Photo of Captain Lee with his first son.

ABOVE: Young Lieutenant Lee at West Point.

BELOW: Portrait of Mary Anne Randolph Custis, daughter of George Washington Parke Custis and wife of Robert E. Lee.

ment to effect repairs to Fort Lafayette, Fort Hamilton, and other parts of the defenses of New York harbor. There he remained for the next five years, with occasional returns to Arlington and Washington and a brief stint on the board of visitors at West Point in June 1844, where he had the opportunity to meet and favorably impress the new commander of the army, Major General Winfield Scott.

Settling down to yet another routine year of repair work in New York, Lee was excited to learn of the plans being made for military expeditions to Mexico. He hoped to be involved, but feared that only line officers would be sent. On August 19, 1846, a delighted Lee received orders to report to Brigadier General John E. Wool in San Antonio, Texas, where he arrived a month later. Wool's instructions were to advance to Chihuahua as part of a blockade of northern Mexico, and a week after his arrival, Lee, now almost 40, found himself for the first time riding with troops against an enemy.

From then until January 1847 there were many alarms, much marching and reconnoitering, bridge-building, and road repair, but not a shot was fired at or by Wool's 6000 troops. In February the war in northern Mexico ended when Santa Anna was routed by General Taylor at Buena Vista, but Lee, at General Winfield

BELOW: Arlington, Lee's home, was selected in 1864 to be the site of a new cemetery for Union Army dead. The grounds became Arlington National Cemetery.

OPPOSITE TOP: Lee's eldest son, George Washington Custis Lee, succeeded his father as head of Washington College, later named Washington and Lee University.

OPPOSITE BOTTOM: The hero of the war with Mexico, General Winfield Scott recognized Lee's contributions to the victory.

BELOW: Agnes Lee, the third daughter of Mary and Robert E. Lee.

Scott's request, had already been ordered to nearby Tampico, where Scott was mounting operations against Vera Cruz and Mexico City. Lee directed battery emplacement for the siege of Vera Cruz. With its surrender after a week of bombardment, Scott advanced toward Cerro Gordo along a route scouted by Lee. In his report of his victory there, General Scott felt compelled to cite the contributions of "R. E. Lee, Engineer"; later, Scott credited Lee's reconnaissance in the campaign in the Valley of Mexico with opening the way to the walls of Mexico City.

On September 13 Lee was slightly wounded while storming the heights of Chapultepec. In Scott's report he won praise for being "as distinguished for felicitous execution as for science and daring." The war had also brought him three brevet promotions, the last to the rank of colonel. After 20 months of service in Mexico, Lee marched his engineering company to Vera Cruz and sailed for home with his professional reputation considerably enhanced.

Lee arrived home at the end of June 1848. In the fall he was assigned to the construction of defensive works in Baltimore to supplement the old Fort McHenry. He remained there until September 1852, when he became ninth superintendent of the U.S. Military Academy. He felt initially unqualified for the post but

discharged it well, making a number of significant improvements to the Academy. But soon again his skills were needed elsewhere.

Owing to the admission of Texas to the Union and the acquisition of New Mexico and other Mexican territory, the nation found it necessary to expand its frontier army to suppress increasing Indian activity. In April 1855 Lee was promoted to a command in the cavalry and, though reluctant to leave the Engineers, he accepted a posting to the Second Cavalry in western Texas, where he commanded squadrons of the regiment at Camp Cooper on the Comanche Reserve. He remained in Texas, putting down Indian forays until the eve of the Civil War.

In November 1857 Colonel Lee had returned briefly to Arlington upon the death of his father-in-law G. W. P. Custis and also for periods in 1858 and 1859 to see to the management of the estate. On October 17, 1859, while in Washington on one of these brief visits, he received a note (carried by Lieutenant J. E. B. Stuart) ordering him – in the absence of General Scott – to report to the Secretary of War. He was then sent at the head of a marine detachment to Harper's Ferry, Virginia, where he was able to capture the notorious John Brown and three other surviving insurgents and effect the safe release of their eleven hostages.

Back in Texas in January 1861, Lee wrote to one of his sons: "The South, in my opinion, had been aggrieved by the acts of the North . . . As an American citizen I . . . would defend any

State if her rights were invaded. But I can anticipate no greater calamity for the country than a dissolution of the Union. It would be an accumulation of all the evils we complain of, and I am willing to sacrifice everything but honor for its preservation.

" . . . Still, a Union that can only be maintained by swords and bayonets, and in which strife and civil war are to take the place of brotherly love and kindness, has no charm for me . . . If the Union is dissolved and the Government disrupted, I shall return to my native State and share the miseries of my people, and save in defense will draw my sword on none."

In February, seven Southern states united to become the Confederate States of America. On April 13 Fort Sumter fell after a 32-hour bombardment, and on the 17th the ordinance of secession was passed; the next day, Lee was asked by an intermediary sent by President Lincoln to take command of all the Union forces. He later wrote:

"I declined the offer [he] made me to take command of the army that was to be brought into the field, stating, as candidly and courteously as I could, that, though opposed to secession and deprecating war, I could take no part in an invasion of the Southern States . . . Upon reflection after returning home, I concluded that I ought no longer to retain any commission I held in the United States army, and on the second morning thereafter I forwarded my resignation to General Scott . . . I then had no other intention than to pass the remainder of my life as a private citizen.

"Two days afterward, on the invitation of the governor of Virginia, I repaired to Richmond . . . and accepted the commission of commander of its forces which was tendered me . . . ."

In June, after Virginia joined the Confederacy, Lee was made one of five full generals. His first orders were to direct the difficult campaign to hold the western counties of Virginia (later West Virginia). In the face of overwhelming Federal forces, he was able to save his units from annihilation, but the western counties were lost and Lee was severely, if unfairly, criticized in the press. After a short tour of the coastal defenses of South Carolina, Georgia, and Florida, Lee was selected by Confederate President Jefferson Davis to be his chief military advisor.

As the Peninsular Campaign of 1862 developed, and Union General George McClellan advanced against General Joseph E. Johnston, Lee helped organize the defenses of Richmond. His genius as a strategist was displayed in the planning of Stonewall Jackson's effective diversionary Shenandoah Valley Campaign. Johnston finally stopped the Federal advance up the Virginia peninsula on May 31 at the battle of Seven Pines (Fair Oaks), but Johnston was seriously wounded and disabled for several months. That evening, President Davis assigned Robert E. Lee to command the Army of Northern Virginia.

BUILT FROM THE RUINS.

LEFT ABOVE: Colonel Lee as superintendent of the United States Military Academy.

ABOVE RIGHT: Engraving of the banner of the South Carolina convention of secession.

LEFT: The fight against John Brown's insurgents at Harper's Ferry. Lee headed a marine detachment that captured Brown.

RIGHT: An early photograph of the interior of Secession Hall in Charleston, South Carolina, birthplace of the Confederate States of America.

Chapter I

The Seven Days' Campaign

BELOW: Lee, as military adviser to Jefferson Davis, addresses the Confederate president and his cabinet in Richmond.

OPPOSITE: Map showing battle-grounds around Richmond. Lee's defenses at Drewry's Bluff (Drury Bluff on the map) on the James River south of the Confederate capital effectively protected the city against the Union fleet.

I n the winter of 1862 the Confederate Congress created the office of "military adviser to the President," with the view of lightening the arduous duties which devolved upon him as commander-in-chief of the Confederate forces. Lee was selected to fill this position, and about the 13th of March, 1862, he entered upon his duties. The staff allowed him consisted of a military secretary with the rank of colonel and four aides with the rank of major. General Lee offered to Major A. L. Long the position of military secretary, and selected for his aides-de-camp Majors Randolph Talcott, Walter H. Taylor, Charles S. Venable, and Charles Marshall. When the writer reported for duty, about the middle of May, he found the general actively engaged in superintending the erection of defences on the James River near Richmond. The battery and obstruc-

tions at Drewry's Bluff were so advanced that the great alarm that had been felt for the safety of the city upon the evacuation of Norfolk began to subside, as there was no longer the fear of an immediate attack. The Federal gunboats had entered the James, and on the 15th the battery at Drewry's Bluff was attacked by the enemy's fleet, consisting of the iron-clads Galena and Naugatuck, a monitor, and two gunboats. These vessels were skilfully handled and gallantly fought. The Galena approached within four hundred yards of the battery, and then opened a spirited fire with her powerful guns; the Naugatuck and monitor closely supported her, while the gunboats delivered their fire at a longer range. After a hotly-contested conflict the fleet was repulsed with heavy loss. The Galena was so severely damaged as to be rendered unfit for future

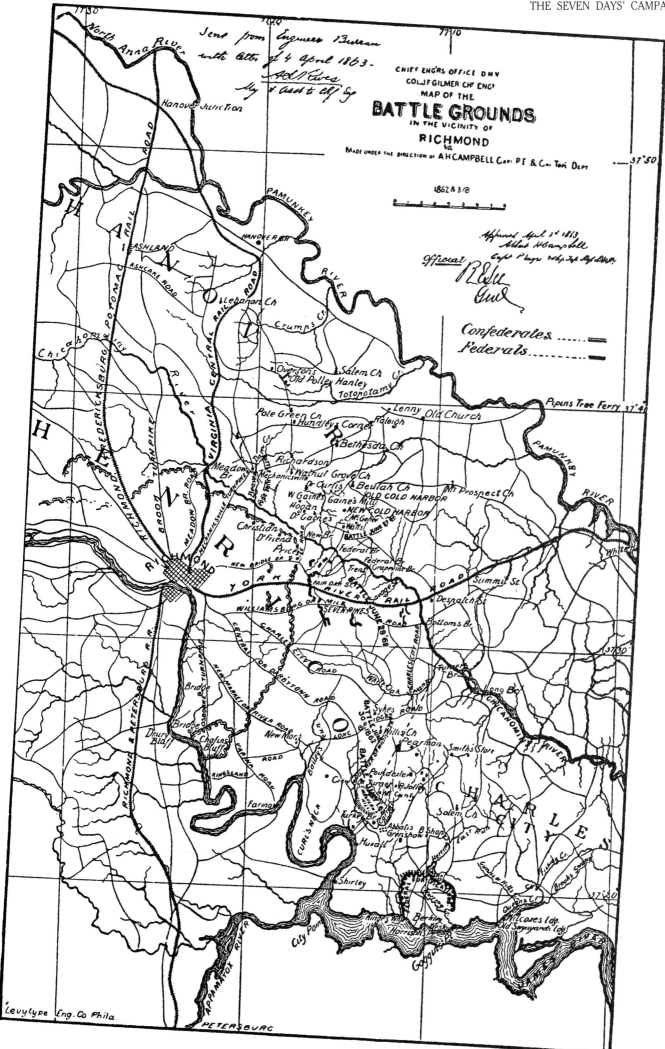

RIGHT: Confederate General Joseph E. Johnston was wounded at the Battle of Seven Pines. President Davis named Lee to replace him as commander of the Army of Northern Virginia.

BELOW: Confederate soldiers wounded in the Battle of Seven Pines are attended by civilians in the streets of Richmond.

service, while the other vessels were more or less injured; the battery sustained but slight damage. This defeat of the gunboats by an incomplete earthwork of only five guns for the first time caused a just value to be placed on defences of that character, which thenceforth became a conspicuous element in defensive operations.

At this time the safety of Richmond was entirely due to the skill and energy of General Lee, for upon the evacuation of Norfolk the James was left enirely open from its mouth to Richmond, and the hastily-constructed defence at Drewry's Bluff was the only barrier interposed between that city and a hostile fleet. After crossing the Chickahominy, about the 20th, General J. E. Johnston assumed the defence of Richmond. He attacked the enemy at Seven Pines on the 31st of May, and was severely wounded, as we have seen, near the close of the action. That event was immediately followed by the appointment of Lee to the command of the Army of Northern Virginia. Though regretting the cause that led to his assignment to the command of the army, he was pleased to be released from the duties of the office for

those of the field, which were far better suited to his active and energetic disposition. He carried with him to the field the same personal staff that had been allowed him in Richmond.

On the afternoon of the 1st of June, General G. W. Smith, on whom the command of the army had devolved when General Johnston was wounded, resigned his command to General Lee, and shortly after retired on account of bad health. It soon appeared that there was considerable depression in the army, the natural consequence of the incidents of war. As some of the officers were apprehensive that the army would not be able to maintain its position should it be attacked, Lee thought it advisable to assemble his principal officers for deliberation on its condition at an early period.

In reference to this point, Mr. Davis, in his *Rise and Fall of the Confederacy*, chap. xxiii., vol. ii., says: "The day after General Lee assumed command I was riding out to the army, when I saw at a house on my left a number of horses, and among them one I recognized as belonging to him. I dismounted and entered the house, where I found him in consultation with a number of his general officers. The tone of the conversation was quite despondent, and one especially pointed out the inevitable consequence of the enemy's advance by throwing out bayoux and constructing successive parallels." Farther on he refers to a want of co-operation that existed among the different divisions during the battle of Fair Oaks and Seven Pines, which was productive of natural distrust that might have resulted in serious demoralization had it not been

ABOVE: Federal reconnaissance balloon *Intrepid* at the Battle of Seven Pines on June 1, 1862.

ABOVE: As the Confederates moved to defend Richmond, they were engaged by Federal troops at Williamsburg on the James.

RIGHT: Union charge at Seven Pines. The Confederate defense, in which General Johnston was wounded, caused the Federals to withdraw temporarily, although they continued to threaten the Southern capital.

speedily corrected. The council met, as had been previously ordered, on the Nine Mile road, near the house which had been occupied by Smith as his headquarters.

The principal officers of the army were present, and were almost unanimous in the opinion that the line then occupied should be abandoned for one nearer Richmond which was considered more defensible.

The line in question was that which had been adopted by Johnston prior to the occupation in force of the south bank of the Chickahominy by the enemy, and was the strongest the country presented; but now the dispirited condition of our troops and the occupation in force by the enemy of the south side of the river caused the most prominent Confederate officers to doubt their ability to hold it, and consequently they urged its evacuation and withdrawal to a position nearer Richmond. Lee thus found himself in a situation of great embarrassment. He did not then possess the fame he was destined soon to acquire. He was also unknown to that army, and lacked its confidence. Under these disadvantages he was obliged to assume the responsibility of maintaining a position pronounced untenable by his principal officers, or of hazarding the safety of Richmond by a withdrawal of his forces that would inevitably result in a forced occupation of the outer defences of the capital and its complete investiture by the enemy, which would have ensured the speedy capture of the city. Lee, who had long been accustomed to rely upon himself, quickly decided on the course to be adopted. It was evident that the present position of the army must be maintained or that Richmond must be abandoned to the enemy, and the loss of Richmond at this time would have been of incalculable injury to the Confederate cause. He therefore, in opposition to the opinion of his subordinates, determined to hold the position in which he found the army; but before making known his determination he made a careful reconnoissance of the whole position, and then declared his intention of holding it, ordering it to be immediately fortified in the most effective manner.

General Lee then reorganized his forces and established a strong defensive line. He selected, with slight alterations, the position then occupied by his troops. This line extended from Chaffin's Bluff, on the James River, crossing the river road about four miles, and the Darby Town, Charles City,

Williamsburg, and Nine Mile roads, about five miles from Richmond to a point on the Chickahominy a little above New Bridge, and then continued up that stream to Meadow Bridge. The army consisted of six divisions. Longstreet's division formed the right, while those of Huger, D. H. Hill, Magruder, Whiting, and A. P. Hill, in the order named, extended to the left. The division of A. P. Hill constituted the left of the Confederate position. The greater part of Stuart's cavalry was on the left, picketing on the Rappahannock and having a small force in observation at Fredericksburg. The duty of constructing a fortified line was apportioned among the divisions, each commander being responsible for the defence in his own front. Very soon a continuous line of breastworks appeared, and as these arose the spirits of the men revived and the sullen silence with which their labor began gave place to jokes and laughter. Those who had entered upon the work with reluctance now felt recompensed by the sense of safety it gave them. The defences daily increased until they were sufficiently strong to resist any attack that was likely to be made upon them. In the mean time the stragglers and convalescents began to return, and the army gradually increased. Lee daily appeared upon the lines, and after a few days his presence inspired the troops with confidence and enthusiasm. McClellan established his headquarters on the south side of the

ABOVE: Union General James B. McClellan's Army of the Potomac faced six entrenched divisions of Lee's Army of Northern Virginia as it crossed the Chickahominy in its advance toward Richmond.

Chickahominy about the same time that Lee assumed the command of the Army of Northern Virginia. The Federal army, after deducting the casualties of the late battle, amounted to about 100,000 men for duty; 75,000 of this force were on the south side of the Chickahominy, the remainder on the north of that stream, extending as high up as Mechanicsville. From this position a junction would be easily formed with McDowell's corps of 40,000 men, which, although a part of McClellan's forces, was persistently held in the neighborhood of Fredericksburg as a covering force for Washington.

* * *

Lee's headquarters at this time were on the Nine Mile road, a position which gave him a good oversight of the army and brought all portions of the lines within easy reach. Yet the batteries, rifle-pits, and earthworks which had been erected with so much labor under his personal supervision were destined to have no further utility than that already adverted to – the infusion of confidence into the previously dispirited army. It was not the purpose of the commanding general to remain upon the defensive and await the slow but sure advances of the enemy. He, on the contrary, formed the bolder decision of hurling the force under his command against the serried battalions of the foe, as indicated in the last-quoted extract from the notebook (*Deleted – Ed.*).

When McClellan crossed the Chickahominy it was thought he would advance immediately upon Richmond. This expectation was disappointed, however, for instead of advancing he began to fortify his position. The right wing rested on the Chickahominy a little below New Bridge, and the left extended to the White Oak Swamp, embracing a front of about four miles, nearly parallel with that of the Confederates. The opposing lines were separated by an interval but little exceeding a mile, but each was obscured from the other's view by the intervening forest. The picket-lines were often within close musket-range of each other. At first there was a good deal of picket-skirmishing, but this was soon discontinued by mutual consent, and a lively exchange of newspapers, coffee, and tobacco succeeded it. The strength of the Confederate force was always greatly over-estimated by McClellan, and his frequent and urgent calls for re-

BELOW: In an engraving made from a field sketch, Federal pickets are shown defending against a Confederate attack as reinforcements arrive.

inforcements exposed his want of confidence in his own strength. General Lee knowing this uneasy, insecure feeling of his antagonist, and McDowell's force, which had always been a thorn in his side, being about this time withdrawn from Fredericksburg for the support of Banks and Shields in the Valley, prepared, as we have said, to assume the offensive. He conceived the bold plan of crossing the Chickahominy, and, attacking the Federal right wing, to force it back and seize McClellan's line of communication with his base of operations. This plan being successfully executed, the Federal general would be compelled to save his army as best he could by retreat. Preparatory to the execution of this plan General J. E. B. Stuart was ordered to make a reconnoissance in the rear of the Federal position. This officer, with a force of about 1000 cavalry, executed his instructions with great boldness and success. He made the entire circuit of the Federal army and gained much important information.

This movement, indeed, was so skilful and brilliant that it has been classed among the most daring cavalry raids ever made. In addition to the information gained he cap-

tured many prisoners and destroyed Federal stores to the value of seven million dollars; and all this with the loss of but a single man, the lamented Captain Latane, who fell while leading a successful charge against a superior force of the enemy. He finally recrossed the Chickahominy, almost in the face of the enemy, with the same intrepidity he had shown at every step of his progress, and with a prestige of daring and success that for years clung to his banner and gained him the reputation of being the most dashing and brilliant cavalry leader of the war.

His design being confirmed by Stuart's successful reconnoissance, Lee proceeded to organize a force requisite for the accomplishment of his proposed enterprise. The troops that could be conveniently spared from North Carolina, South Carolina, and Georgia were ordered to Richmond. By the 20th of June, Major-general T. H. Holmes, with 6000 men from North Carolina; Brigadier-general Ripley, with 6000 from South Carolina; and Brigadier-general Lawton, with 5000 from Georgia, had arrived in Richmond. At the same time General Jackson was ordered to withdraw secretly from the Valley and proceed with such expedition as

LEFT: In his plans to assume the offensive against McClellan, General Lee included the 6000 soldiers from South Carolina commanded by Brigadier General Roswell Ripley.

ABOVE: Union General Fitz John Porter, commanding troops north of the Chickahominy, was forced by Lee to abandon his position at Gaines's Mill and rejoin McClellan's main army on the south side of the river.

would enable him to reach Hanover Junction by the afternoon of the 25th of June. In order to mask his designs from the Federals, Lee directed Whiting's division and Lawton's brigade to proceed to Staunton, apparently with the view of reinforcing Jackson, but really under orders to return immediately and join that general on the 25th at Hanover Junction. This movement further strengthened McClellan in his opinion of Lee's vastly superior force, and completely blinded him in regard to the real intentions of that general.

General Lee determined to attack the Federal right wing on the morning of the 26th of June. Jackson was directed to move to Atlee's Station on the Central Railroad. A. P. Hill was directed to cross the Chickahominy at Meadow Bridge as soon as Jackson arrived in supporting distance, attack the Federals at Mechanicsville, and drive them from that place, so that the bridge on the Richmond and Mechanicsville road might be open for the advance of the other troops; Longstreet and D. H. Hill were ordered to move their divisions as near as practicable to the Mechanicsville bridge without discovering themselves to the observation of the Federals; while Magruder, Huger, and Holmes held the lines that were now completed, with instructions to watch closely the

movements of the enemy in their front and act as circumstances might suggest. The effective force of the Army of Northern Virginia, including that brought by Jackson from the Valley, as shown by the field returns of June 24th or 25th, amounted to a little more than 81,000 men: 30,000 of these were left in observation under Magruder, while Lee led 50,000 to the attack of the Federal force north of the Chickahominy, which amounted to about 25,000 men, commanded by Fitz John Porter. One division of this force, about 6000 or 7000 strong, under the command of General J. F. Reynolds, occupied Mechanicsville at the extreme right of the Federal position. The main body, under the immediate command of Porter, was posted near Cold Harbor or Gaines's Mill, about six miles below Mechanicsville, and connected by bridges with the main body of the Federal army south of the Chickahominy.

Jackson, having bivouacked at Ashton on the night of the 25th, and his men being fatigued by previous long marches, did not reach his designated position in line of battle until the afternoon of the 26th. This delay was very embarrassing to Lee, and greatly increased the difficulty of executing his plan of operations, as it exposed his design to the enemy and allowed him time to prepare for the approaching storm. General A. P. Hill, on the arrival of Jackson – about four o'clock – crossed the Chickahominy and made a spirited attack on the Federal force at Mechanicsville and compelled it to retire to a position which had been previously prepared beyond the Beaver Dam, a small stream about one mile south-east of the village. The way being now open, the divisions of Longstreet and D. H. Hill began to cross the Chickahominy. Ripley's brigade, which was the first to cross, was ordered to support A. P. Hill in his attempt to dislodge the Federals from their new position. Failing in their first attempt to dislodge them, the approach of night prevented any other being made to carry their position. Reynolds, finding his position would be turned, retired during the night to Gaines's Mill. On the morning of the 27th, Lee formed his army into three columns. The division of A. P. Hill, forming the centre, moved by the main road from Mechanicsville to Gaines's Mill; Longstreet moved by a road between this and the Chickahominy; while Jackson and D. H. Hill moved by a road to the left which intersected the Mechanicsville road a mile and a half beyond Gaines's Mill or Cold Harbor. Stuart with his cavalry covered the left flank of the army as it advanced. The guide, having received indefinite instructions from Jackson, led his column by a road that intersected with the Mechanicsville road before reaching Gaines's Mill. This brought the head of Jackson's column against Hill's troops. Jackson, being obliged to countermarch in order to gain the right road, caused a delay of several hours in the operations of General Lee and materially affected his plan of attack. It was his intention that when Jackson reached the Mechanicsville road he should form his troops in order of battle and attack the Federal right, while A. P. Hill attacked the centre and Longstreet the left.

The Federal position near Gaines's Mill was a plateau bounded on the north-west side by a bluff eighty or ninety feet in elevation, which, curving to the north and east, gradually diminished into a gentle slope. The plateau was bounded on its north side by a stream flowing along its base, whose banks gradually widened and deepened until, when reaching the bluff, they had gained the width of eight or ten and the depth of five or six feet, thus forming a natural ditch. Three lines of breastworks, rising one above the other, had been constructed upon the base of the bluff, and its crest was crowned with artillery. Three lines of Federal infantry occupied the bluff, and one line extended along the north-east crest for more than a mile, and batteries of artillery were in position in rear of the infantry. The Federal position was very strong, and to carry it required the greatest bravery and resolution on the part of the assailants. McClellan, being now aware of Lee's real design, reinforced Porter, increasing his force to about 40,000 men. When the columns of Hill and Longstreet had arrived in easy attacking-distance, General Lee caused them to halt in order to give Jackson time to gain his position. Waiting until one o'clock, Lee ordered Longstreet and A. P. Hill to commence the attack. The Confederate skirmishers advanced and drove in the Federal pickets. While the column of Longstreet advanced by the road to Dr. Gaines's house, and that of Hill by the main Mechanicsville

ABOVE: General Ambrose P. Hill, a Virginian, was one of Lee's most dependable lieutenants.

BELOW: General Robert E. Lee's headquarters during the battles at Gaines's Mill.

road, the Federal position was hidden from Hill by the intervening woods. Deploying several regiments to support his skirmishers, he pushed them through the woods. Very soon the Federal line was developed by a heavy fire of musketry. Hill's column then deployed and advanced to the attack on the Federal centre.

When Longstreet arrived at Gaines's house he was in full view of the Federal left. Taking advantage of an intervening ridge, the crest of which was parallel with and about three hundred yards from the Federal lines, he deployed his troops under its cover. Hearing Hill's attack, Longstreet approached to gain the Federal left. His first line on reaching the crest of the ridge was met by a storm of shot and shell; without faltering it swept down the slope toward the Federal position in the face of a terrible fire of artillery and musketry until arrested by the wide and steep banks of the stream at the foot. Being unable to cross it, this line was obliged to fall back. These troops, although much cut up, re-formed for a second attack. Several Confederate batteries were served with considerable effect in covering the advance of the infantry. D. H. Hill, on reaching the scene of action, took position on the left of A. P. Hill and engaged the enemy. The battle having become general, General Lee sent several staff officers to bring up Jack-

son's troops to the support of Hill and Longstreet. Whiting's division and Lawton's brigade were the first to arrive. Whiting was directed to fill the interval between Longstreet and A. P. Hill, and Lawton was sent to the left of D. H. Hill to engage the Federal right. Generals Ewell, Elzey, and Winder, as they arrived, were sent to the support of the Hills, and one brigade was sent to the support of Longstreet. Jackson led in person the remainder of his troops against the Federal right. The battle had raged with great fury for more than two hours, and the Federal lines seemed as unshaken as when it first began. The Confederates had been repulsed in several attempts to force them. The day was now drawing to a close, and Lee decided to end the conflict by a charge of the whole line. The word "Charge!" as it passed along the line, was responded to by a wild shout and an irresistible rush on the Federal position. The Texas brigade, led by the gallant Hood, was the first to penetrate the Federal works. It was immediately followed by other regiments, and in a few minutes the whole position was carried and the plateau was covered with a mass of fugitives. The Federals were in full flight, pursued by the Confederates, who delivered deadly volleys at every step.

While General Lee was attacking Porter's position at Gaines's Mill, Magruder made a

BELOW: The earliest known use of railway artillery was that by a battery under Confederate General John B. Magruder during the battles around Richmond. The idea is believed to have been first outlined in a letter from General Lee to the chief of the Ordnance Department on June 5, 1862.

spirited demonstration against that of McClellan on the south side of the Chickahominy. This double attack served to bewilder McClellan, and caused him to withhold reinforcements that would otherwise have been sent to Porter. This battle is considered by many as the most stubbornly-contested battle of the war. It is true that the troops on both sides displayed great valor and determination, and proved themselves worthy of the nation to which they belonged. Porter deserves much credit for the skilful selection of his position and the gallant manner in which he defended it. The victory was complete. When night closed the Confederates were in undisputed possession of the field. The next morning Lee directed Stuart with his cavalry, supported by Ewell's division of infantry, to seize the York River Railroad. McClellan was thus cut off from his base of supplies, and reduced to the necessity of retreating by one of two routes – the one by the Peninsula, the other by the James River, under the cover of the gunboats. He chose the latter as the shortest and easiest.

General Lee remained on the 28th on the north side of the Chickahominy in observation of McClellan's movements. Instructions were sent at the same time to Magruder to keep a vigilant watch on the Federals and without delay report any movement that might be discovered. These instructions were not as faithfully executed as they should have been, for the retreat of the Federals had commenced on the morning of the 28th, and was not discovered until the morning of the 29th, when the Federal lines were found by two engineer officers, Captains Meade and Johnston, to be abandoned, although the Confederate pickets were in many places less than half a mile from the Federal lines.

The safe retreat of McClellan to the James is mainly due to the advantage thus gained. When General Lee on the morning of the 29th found that the Federal army was in retreat he ordered an immediate pursuit. All of the troops on the north of the Chickahominy, with the exception of the divisions of Ewell and Jackson, and Stuart's cavalry, which were to remain in observation lest the Federals might change their line of retreat, were ordered to recross that stream with the view of overtaking the retreating columns. General Lee on recrossing the Chickahominy found Magruder, Huger, and Holmes preparing to pursue the retreating Federal army. At twelve o'clock the pursuit

was commenced, and about three Magruder came upon Sumner's corps, which was in position near Savage's Station. General Heintzelman having retired, Sumner's and Franklin's corps had to receive Magruder's attack unsupported. Sumner held his position with great obstinacy until night ended the conflict. This determined stand enabled the Federal army to make a safe passage of the White Oak Swamp. In the afternoon of the 29th, Jackson was directed to cross the Chickahominy and relieve Magruder in the pursuit. Lee directed the other divisions of his army to march by several roads leading in the direction of McClellan's line of retreat, with the view of striking his column in the flank while Jackson pressed him in the rear. About three o'clock on the 30th, Lee, with the divisions of Longstreet and A. P. Hill, struck the Federal column at Frazier's Farm, and a fierce combat ensued which was

ABOVE: Confederate soldiers charge a Union battery in the Battle of Frazier's Farm on June 30.

BELOW: Union General Philip Kearney's division at White Oak Swamp on June 30 supported McClellan's withdrawal to a safe position on Malvern Hill.

closely contested until night. Contrary to his expectations, he was not supported in this attack by Generals Jackson and Huger, consequently McClellan again escaped and continued his retreat during the night to Malvern Hill.

The delay on the part of General Jackson was very unusual. The explanation of his delay on this occasion was that, being greatly exhaused by long marches and battles for more than a week, he sought a short repose. His staff, out of mistaken regard for their general, permitted him to sleep far beyond the time he had allowed himself. When he awoke he was greatly chagrined at the loss of time that had occurred, the damage of which he was unable to repair. Though General Lee accomplished all that was at first proposed, yet had the parts assigned to some of his subordinates been performed with the exactness that was naturally expected, the results of his operations would have been far greater than those shown in the sequel.

On the morning of the 1st of July it was discovered that McClellan had occupied in force the strong position of Malvern Hill, while his powerful artillery swept every approach, and the shot of the gunboats fell beyond the Confederate lines. After a careful reconnoissance of McClellan's position, Lee determined to attack his left. His first line, composed of the divisions of Magruder, D. H. Hill, and Jackson, was advanced under cover of the wood near the base of the hill. Magruder was ordered to attack the Federal left, while Hill and Jackson threatened their centre and right. The attack was delayed until near sundown, when Magruder made a most gallant assault. By dint of hard fighting his troops gained the crest of the hill and

forced back the Federal left, but were in turn driven back. The firing continued along the line until ten o'clock. The Confederates lay upon their arms where the battle closed, ready to resume the fight as soon as the daylight should appear.

Under the cover of the night McClellan secretly retired, his retreat being facilitated by a heavy fall of rain, which deadened the sound of his withdrawal. The Confederates the next morning, groping through the dense fog, came upon the abandoned lines. This was the first information they had of the retreat. McClellan had now gained the protection of the Federal gunboats; therefore Lee did not immediately pursue, but ordered a day's rest, which the troops greatly needed. McClellan continued his retreat to Harrison's Landing on the James River, where he took up a position. Lee advanced the next day to that neighborhood and after a careful reconnoissance of the Federal lines deemed it inadvisable to attack, and, as there was no probability of the Army of the Potomac speedily resuming operations, he returned to his former camp near Richmond to rest, recruit, and reorganize his army.

While in the vicinity of Harrison's Landing the attack of Colonel J. Thompson Brown's artillery upon the Federal gunboats afforded a brilliant episode to the last scene of the military drama that had just been acted.

The loss sustained by both armies during the recent operations was considerable; that, however, caused by exhaustion and illness probably equalled the casualties of actual battle. The number of Confederate killed and wounded amounted to about 10,000, whilst the Federal loss exceeded this. Reviewing the operations that have just been described, we cannot fail to observe

BELOW: Union artillery under General Henry W. Slocum engages Confederates on the Charles City Road as General McClellan retreats to Harrison's Landing on the James River.

the important results achieved by the skill and energy of an able commander. On the 1st of June, General Lee assumed the command of an army that did not exceed 50,000 men. With this force he erected defences to withstand any attack that might be made against them, and besides in less than a month increased his army to 80,000 men, without giving up one foot of territory and without endangering either public or private property. He also raised its discipline and spirit to such a height that he was enabled to take the offensive and force his adversary, notwithstanding his superiority of numbers and the finely-appointed state of his army, to abandon a base of operations that had occupied almost the exclusive attention of his Government for more than a year, incurring in doing so a heavy loss of material.

McClellan, after establishing himself at Harrison's Landing, called for large reinforcements to enable him to resume active operations. It was decided to order Burnside from North Carolina to reinforce the Army of the Potomac. When Lee re-

gained his former camp near Richmond he immediately set about reorganizing his army. His victory over McClellan had filled the Confederacy with joy, and the men who had left the army a short time before broken down and depressed returned full of spirit and energy.

Before the end of July the Army of Northern Virginia, with the addition of one or two brigades from South Carolina and Georgia, numbered about 70,000 effective men. This army, having to a great extent supplied itself by captures from the Federal army, was better armed and equipped than it had previously been.

Lee had formed it into two corps, giving one to Longstreet and the other to Jackson, officers who had proved themselves fully worthy of the important commands conferred upon them.

As . . . we progress with our narrative it will be seen to what distinction each rose in defence of the Southern Confederacy.

* * *

ABOVE: Soldiers of the Third Georgia Infantry. The two at right, half brothers, died at Malvern Hill.

Chapter II

Second Bull Run

Great ... must have been the disappointment at Washington, after such glorious prospects, on witnessing the precipitate retreat of the Federal army on which such high hopes had been centred ... As there was no probability of McClellan's immediately resuming active operations against Richmond, Lee determined, by assuming the offensive and threatening the Federal capital, to force him to make an entire change in his plan of campaign. With that view he despatched Jackson with three divisions of infantry and a proportionate amount of artillery to the neighborhood of Gordonsville, while remaining himself at Richmond with Longstreet's corps, D. H. Hill's and Anderson's divisions of infantry, and Stuart's cavalry in observation of McClellan, who was now slowly recovering from the stuning effect of his defeat.

*   *   *

About the 1st of August, the advance of the Federal army having reached Culpeper Court-house, Jackson moved to the Rapidan

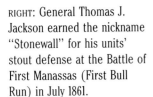

and took a position in the vicinity of Orange Court-house ... The forces under Banks, Fremont, and McDowell, ... were formed into an army, the command of which was given to General Pope.

*   *   *

About the time that Jackson reached the Rapidan, Pope arrived at Culpeper Court-house, and extended his advance corps toward the Rapidan. The Federal cavalry finding the Rapidan occupied by the Confederates, the leading corps took up a position along a range of low hills near Cedar Mountain, about four miles west of Culpeper Court-house. Having learned that a part of the Federal force had not arrived there, Jackson determined to attack Pope before his army could be united. He therefore secretly recrossed the Rapidan, and by a rapid movement on the 9th of August gained the position near Cedar Mountain before the

Federals were aware of his design. The battle was hotly contested for several hours, when the Federals were defeated and driven back to Culpeper Court-house. Jackson . . . then recrossed the Rapidan.

*　　*　　*

The advance of Jackson to Gordonsville, above mentioned, and his subsequent advance upon the position of General Pope near Culpeper Court-house, caused the Federal authorities to determine upon the immediate withdrawal of the Army of the Potomac from the James . . . General Lee . . . divined, with the intuition of genius, that his presence and that of his army could be spared from the immediate vicinity of Richmond, and might be able to teach General Pope that the road to New Orleans was "a hard road to travel." Preliminary to future operations he sent forward Longstreet's corps to join Jackson in the vicinity of Gordonsville, and about the middle of August proceeded in person to assume the direction of affairs in that quarter.

On reaching the locality of the projected movements he found Jackson occupying the line of the Rapidan, while Longstreet's force was encamped in the neighborhood of Gordonsville. The army, including Stuart's cavalry, at this time amounted to 65,000 effective men, while the opposing army of Pope numbered 50,000, and occupied a position between Culpeper Court-house and the Rapidan.

Lee at once determined to assume the offensive, and with that purpose in view he moved his whole army below Orange Court-house to a position south of Clark's Mountain, where he could avail himself of the fords of the Rapidan on the flanks of the Federal army. He reached this position on August 17th, the movement having been effected, under cover of the forest, without the knowledge of General Pope.

The absence of Stuart's cavalry delayed the army in this position till the morning of the 20th, and enabled Pope – who, through an unlucky accident, became aware of the movement of his shrewd adversary – to beat a hasty retreat . . . On the 18th, Lee and his staff ascended Clark's Mountain, and reconnoitered the Federal position. In plain view before them lay Pope's army, stretched out in fancied security, and to all appearance in utter ignorance of the vicinity of a powerful foe . . . On the afternoon of the 19th the signal-station on the top of the mountain not-

ABOVE: Federals at the Battle of Cedar Mountain, the start of the Second Manassas (Second Bull Run) campaign, on August 9, 1862.

ified the Confederate commander that a change had occurred in the situation of affairs. The enemy had evidently taken the alarm ... As it afterward appeared, Pope had learned of Lee's vicinity through the capture of Lieutenant Fitzhugh of Stuart's staff, on whom had been found a letter revealing the fact of the movement of the Confederate army. On gaining this important and somewhat startling information, he had immediately given orders to break camp and retreat in all haste to the line of the Rappahannock ....

The retreating Federal army was followed by Lee in rapid pursuit, but it had crossed the Rappahannock by the time he reached the vicinity of that stream. Pope on crossing the river took up a position on the left bank, his left covering Rappahannock Station, his right extending in the direction of Warrenton Springs. Lee confronted him on the right bank of the river ....

When it became known at Washington that Pope had been compelled to retreat and recross the Rappahannock, the Federal authorities made every effort to rapidly reinforce him by troops drawn from the Army of the Potomac and from Burnside's force, which had been withdrawn from North Carolina. General Lee, in order to retard the forwarding of troops and supplies to the Federal army, ordered Stuart to turn Pope's right, gain his rear, inflict as much damage as he could upon the Orange and Alexandria Railroad, and gain information of the enemy's movements. Stuart, in compliance with his instructions, crossed the Rappahannock late in the afternoon of the 21st, a few

BELOW: Northern black troops and Virginia civilians follow Union General Pope's retreat across the Rappahannock.

miles above Warrenton Springs, with a brigade of cavalry, and, screening his movement by the mountain-spurs and intervening forests, he proceeded toward the village of Warrenton, passing that place after nightfall, and advanced direct upon Catlett's Station on the railroad. Arriving in the midst of a violent storm, he surprised and captured the Federal encampment at that place, which he found to contain General Pope's headquarters. He secured Pope's letter-book and papers with many other valuable articles.

On account of the heavy fall of rain the timbers of the railroad bridge at Catlett's were so saturated with water that Stuart was unable to burn it, and, being pressed for time, he failed to greatly damage the railroad. He returned, bringing with him his valuable booty, without the loss of a man. By the capture of Pope's papers Lee gained an accurate knowledge of the situation of the Federal army. Acting on it, he ordered Jackson to advance his corps to Jeffersonton and secure the bridge over the Rappahannock at Warrenton Springs. Jackson moved up the river, leaving his train to follow under the escort of Trimble's brigade. The Federals, being tempted by the appearance of a large train in their vicinity, sent a strong detachment to intercept it. Trimble, reinforced by Hood's brigade of Longstreet's corps, met this detachment, and after a fierce combat drove it back with heavy loss. Jackson, on arriving at Jeffersonton in the afternoon of the 22nd found that the bridge on the Warrenton turnpike had been destroyed by the

ABOVE: Station on the Orange and Alexandria Railroad at Warrenton, Virginia. Here Jeb Stuart discovered Pope's plans for the disposition of Federal troops.

Federals. The river being low, he succeeded in sending Early's brigade with one of Lawton's Georgia regiments across the river on an old mill-dam to act as a corps of observation. During the night the river was made impassable by heavy rains. The next day, the Federals beginning to appear in great force, Early with great dexterity took a position in a wood adjacent to the river, so as to effectually conceal his lack of strength. The river having fallen during the day, he recrossed at night without loss. The Federals burned the railroad bridge of Rappahannock Station, and moved their left higher up the river. On the 23rd, Lee ordered Longstreet's corps to follow Jackson and mass in the vicinity of Jeffersonton. The headquarters of the army was also moved to that place.

* * *

General Longstreet made a feint on the position of Warrenton on the morning of the 24th, under cover of which Jackson's corps was withdrawn from the front to the vicinity of the road from Jeffersonton to the upper fords of the Rappahannock. Jackson was then directed to make preparation to turn the Federal position and seize their communications about Manassas Junction. Longstreet continued his cannonade at intervals throughout the day, to which the Federals replied with increasing vigor, showing that Pope was massing his army in Lee's front.

It was the object of Lee to hold Pope in his present position by deluding him with the belief that it was his intention to force a passage of the river at that point, until Jackson by a flank movement could gain his rear. Longstreet, on the morning of the 25th, resumed his cannonade with increased energy, and at the same time made a display of infantry above and below the bridge. Jackson then moved up the river to a ford eight miles above; crossing at that point and turning eastward, by a rapid march he reached the vicinity of Salem. Having made a march of twenty-five miles, he bivouacked for the night. Stuart's cavalry covered his right flank, the movement being masked by the natural features of the country. The next morning at dawn the march was resumed by the route through Thoroughfare Gap.

The cavalry, moving well to the right, passed around the west end of Bull Run Mountain and joined the infantry at the village of Gainesville, a few miles from the Orange and Alexandria Railroad. Pressing forward, still keeping the cavalry well to the right, Jackson struck the railroad at Bristoe Station late in the afternoon, where he captured two empty trains going east. After dark he sent a detachment under Stuart to secure Manassas Junction, the main dépôt of supplies of the Federal army. The cavalry moved upon the flanks of this position, while the infantry, commanded by Trimble, assaulted the works in front and carried them with in-

OPPOSITE: Two photographers lunching in the field before the Second Battle of Bull Run.

BELOW: Erecting Confederate fortifications at Manassas. The Second Bull Run campaign ran from August 9 until September 2.

significant loss, capturing two batteries of light artillery with their horses and a detachment of 300 men, besides an immense amount of army supplies. The next morning, after effectually destroying the railroad at Bristoe, Jackson left Ewell with his division and a part of Stuart's cavalry to retard the Federals if they should advance in that direction, and moved his main body to Manassas, where he allowed his troops a few hours to refresh themselves upon the abundant stores that had been captured. About twelve o'clock the sound of artillery in the direction of Bristoe announced the Federal advance. Not having transportation to remove the captured supplies, Jackson directed his men to take what they could carry off, and ordered the rest to be destroyed.

General Ewell, having repulsed the advance of two Federal columns, rejoined Jackson at Manassas. The destruction of the captured stores having been completed, Jackson retired with his whole force to Bull Run and took a position for the night, a part of his troops resting on the battle-field of the previous year. Pope, on hearing of the interruption of his communications, sent a force to get information of the extent of the damage that had been done to the railroad.

Upon learning that Jackson was in his rear, he immediately abandoned his position on the Rappahannock and proceeded with all despatch to intercept him before he could be reinforced by Lee. His advance having been arrested on the 27th by Ewell, he did not proceed beyond Bristoe that day. Lee on the 26th withdrew Longstreet's corps from its position in front of Warrenton Springs, covering the withdrawal by a small rearguard and artillery, and directed it to follow Jackson by the route he had taken the day before. The trains were ordered to move by the same route and to keep closed on Longstreet's corps.

* * *

The corps bivouacked for the night in the vicinity of Salem. On the morning of the succeeding day, the 27th, a messenger appeared bringing the important and cheering news of the success of Jackson at Bristoe and Manassas. These tidings were received with enthusiasm by the soldiers, who, animated with high hopes of victory, pressed on with the greatest energy, and that evening reached the plains a few miles west of Thoroughfare Gap, in the Bull Run Mountains, through which Jackson's

BELOW: A column of the Union Army of the Potomac crossing Kettle Run, above Warrenton.

column had passed a few days previously.

Thoroughfare Gap was reached about noon of the 28th. It was quickly found to be occupied by a Federal force. Some slight attempt was made to dislodge the enemy, but without success, as their position proved too strong, and it seemed as if the movement of the Confederate army in that direction was destined to be seriously interfered with. Meanwhile, nothing further had been heard from Jackson, and there was a natural anxiety in regard to his position and possible peril. Unless the mountains could speedily be passed by Longstreet's corps the force under Jackson might be assailed by the whole of Pope's army, and very severely dealt with.

Under these critical circumstances General Lee made every effort to find some available route over the mountains, sending reconnoissances to right and left in search of a practicable pass. Some of the officers ascended the mountain during the evening, and perceived from its summit a large force which lay in front of the Gap. Meanwhile, the sound of cannonading was audible from the other side of the range, and it was evident that an engagement was taking place.

*   *   *

Fortunately, circumstances favored the Confederate cause. One of the reconnoitering parties found a woodchopper, who told them of an old road over the mountain to which he could guide them, and which might be practicable for infantry. Hood was at once directed to make an effort to lead his division across the mountain by this route. This he succeeded in doing, and the head of his column reached the other side of the range by morning. Another route had also been discovered by which Wilcox was enabled to turn the Gap.

In the mean time, Pope himself had been playing into the hands of his adversary. He had ordered McDowell to retire from the Gap and join him to aid in the anticipated crushing of Jackson. McDowell did so, leaving Rickett's division to hold the Gap. In evident ignorance of the vicinity of Longstreet's corps, this force was also withdrawn during the night, and on the morning of the 29th Lee found the Gap unoccupied, and at once marched through at the head of Longstreet's column. On reaching Gainesville, three miles beyond the Gap, he found Stuart, who informed him of Jackson's situation. The division was at once marched into position

on Jackson's right.

Pope had unknowingly favored the advance of the Confederate commander. His removal of McDowell from his position had been a tactical error of such magnitude that it could not well be retrieved. The object of the movement had been to surround Jackson at Manassas Junction, upon which place the several corps of the army were marching by various routes. Pope wrote in his order to McDowell, "If you will march promptly and rapidly at the earliest dawn upon Manassas Junction, we shall bag the whole crowd." The scheme was a good one, but for two unconsidered contingencies. Had Jackson awaited the enemy at Manassas Junction, he would have found himself in a trap. But he did not choose to do so. When the van of the Federal columns reached the Junction, they found that the bird had flown. And Longstreet's corps,

ABOVE: In an engraving from a field drawing by A. R. Waud, General Robert E. Lee is seen observing the skirmishing at Thoroughfare Gap.

BELOW: General McDowell's camp at Manassas. The Union force arrived too late at Manassas Junction to trap the forewarned General Jackson.

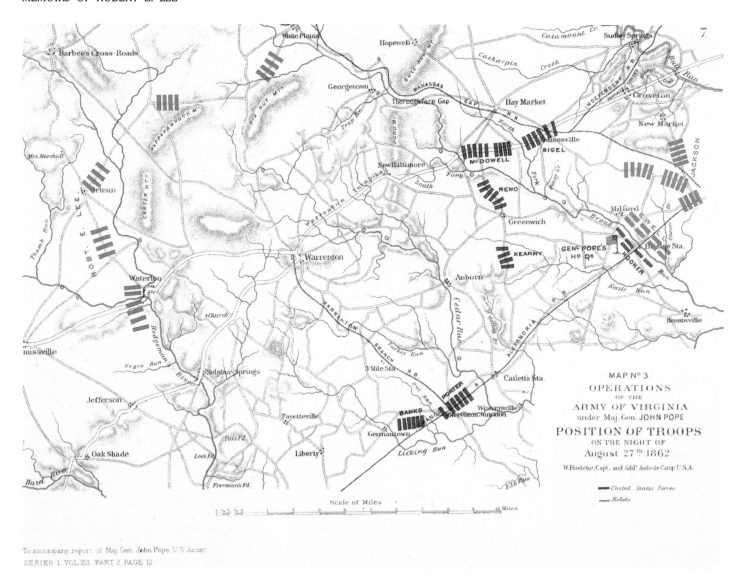

To accompany report of Maj Gen John Pope U S Army
SERIES 1 VOL XII. PART 2 PAGE 12.

ABOVE: Map accompanying Pope's report on the battles records the positions of troops on both sides on the night of August 27.

OPPOSITE TOP: Map showing the action of August 28.

OPPOSITE BOTTOM: A Currier & Ives print attempts to show the ferocity of the fighting at Bull Run on August 29.

which might have been prevented from passing the Bull Run range, had been given free opportunity to cross to the aid of Jackson, who on the night of the 27th and morning of the 28th left the Junction and made a rapid march to the westward. The error was a fatal one to the hopes of the boasting Western general.

The cannonade at the Gap on the 28th had informed Jackson of Lee's proximity. He at once took a position north of the Warrenton turnpike, his left resting on Bull Run, near Sudley Church, and his right extending toward Gainesville. The distance of this position from the Warrenton road varied from one to two miles, the greater part of the left embracing a railroad cut, while the centre and right occupied a commanding ridge. In this position Jackson could easily unite with Lee on his passing Thoroughfare Gap, or, failing in that and being hard pressed, he could retire by the east end of Bull Run Mountain and unite with Lee on the north side of that mountain. The divisions of Ewell and Taliaferro formed the right and

centre of Jackson's line of battle, while that of A. P. Hill constituted his left. Jackson had barely completed his arrangements when a heavy column of Federal infantry (King's division of McDowell's corps) appeared on the Warrenton turnpike. In order to delay its advance several batteries were placed in position, which by a well-directed fire caused them to halt; at the same time Jackson ordered Taliaferro to deploy one brigade across the Warrenton turnpike, holding his other brigades in reserve. Ewell was directed to support him. About three o'clock the Federals bore down in heavy force upon Ewell and Taliaferro, who maintained their positions with admirable firmness, repelling attack after attack until night. The loss on both sides was considerable. Among the wounded on the side of the Confederates were Generals Taliaferro and Ewell, the latter seriously, having to lose his leg.

Jackson, with barely 20,000 men, now found himself confronted by the greater part of the Federal army. Any commander with less firmness would have sought safety in

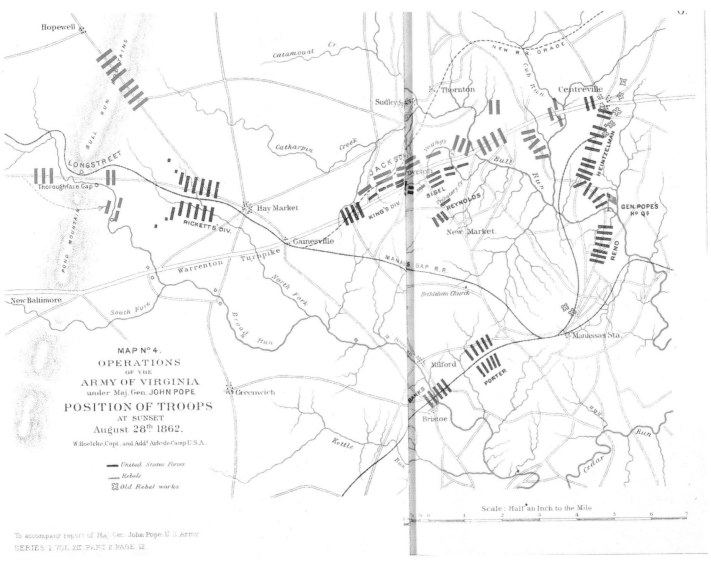

MAP Nº 4.
OPERATIONS
OF THE
ARMY OF VIRGINIA
under Maj. Gen. JOHN POPE
POSITION OF TROOPS
AT SUNSET
August 28ᵗʰ 1862.

W. Hoelcke, Capt. and Addᵗ Aide-de-Camp U.S.A.

United States Forces
Rebels
Old Rebel works.

Scale : Half an Inch to the Mile

To accompany report of Maj. Gen. John Pope, U.S. Army
SERIES 1 VOL. XII. PART 2 PAGE 12.

ABOVE: Ruins of Stone Bridge on the blasted battlefield at Bull Run.

retreat. But having heard the Confederate guns at Thoroughfare Gap, he knew that Lee would join him the next day. Therefore he determined to hold his position at all hazards.

By the morning of the 29th, as we have already described, Hood's division had reached the south side of the mountain, and early in the day was joined by the remainder of Longstreet's corps by way of the open Gap.

While these important movements were in progress, Pope had resumed his attack upon Jackson, and was pressing him with his whole force, hoping to crush him before he could be relieved by Lee. On the arrival of Lee, Pope discontinued his attack, and retired to the position which the year before had been the scene of the famous battle of Bull Run, or Manassas. Lee then took a position opposite, with Longstreet's corps occupying a lower range of hills extending across and at right angles to the Warrenton turn-

pike, while Jackson occupied the line of railroad before mentioned, which, slightly deviating from the general direction of Longstreet's position, formed with it an obtuse crotchet, opening toward the enemy. An elevated ridge connecting Jackson's right with Longstreet's left, forming the centre of the Confederate position, was strongly occupied with artillery to fill the interval between Longstreet and Jackson. The hills on the right, were crowned by the Washington Artillery, commanded by Colonel Walton. The remainder of the artillery was distributed at prominent points throughout the line, while Stuart's cavalry covered its flanks and observed the movements of the enemy. Since Pope's retreat from Culpeper Courthouse he had been frequently reinforced by detachments from the armies of McClellan and Burnside. The greater part of those armies having now joined him, and the remainder being in supporting-distance, his arrogance revived, and, being sure of an easy victory, he sent the most sanguine despatches to the authorities at Washington. In preparation for battle he took a position embracing a succession of low ridges, nearly parallel to, and about a mile from, the line assumed by Lee. About midway between the two armies lay a narrow valley, through which meandered a small brook, whose low murmurs seemed to invite the weary soldier to slake his thirst with its cool and limpid waters. The afternoon of the 29th was principally occupied in preparation. Longstreet's corps, on the right, was formed in two lines. Jackson, on the left, having been considerably reduced by rapid marching and hard fighting, could present only a single line with a small reserve.

On the morning of the 30th an ominous silence pervaded both armies. Each seemed to be taking the measure of its antagonist.

Lee saw threatening him the armies of Pope, McClellan, and Burnside, whose combined strength exceeded 150,000 men, while his own army was less than 60,000 strong. Notwithstanding this disparity of numbers, the presence of Lee, Jackson, and Longstreet inspired the troops with confidence far exceeding their numerical strength. About eight o'clock the Federal batteries opened a lively cannonade upon the Confederate centre, which was responded to with spirit by the battalions of Colonel Stephen D. Lee and Major Shoemaker. This practice having continued for an hour, both sides relapsed into silence. This was the prelude to the approaching contest. Between twelve and one o'clock the cannonade was resumed in earnest. The thunder of cannon shook the hills, while shot and shell, shrieking and hissing, filled the air, and the sulphurous

BELOW: Men of Company C, 41st New York Infantry at Manassas before the start of the battles. In a month, a total of 25,000 Union and Confederate soldiers who took part in the Second Bull Run campaign would be dead, wounded or missing.

smoke, settling in black clouds along the intervening valley, hung like a pall over the heavy columns of infantry which rushed into the "jaws of death." Pope, having directed his principal attack upon the Confederate left, advanced his infantry in powerful force against Jackson, whose single line behind the friendly shelter of railroad cuts and embankments received this mighty array with tremendous volleys of musketry, hurling back line after line, only to be replaced by fresh assailants. Each moment the conflict became closer and more deadly. At times the roar of musketry gave place to the clash of bayonets, and at one point, after the Confederates had exhausted their ammunition, the assailants were repelled with stones which had been thrown up from a neighboring excavation. At the critical moment when the fate of Jackson's corps was trembling in the balance, Colonel Lee dashed with his artillery into a position that enfiladed the Federal right wing and hurled upon it a storm of shot and shell. At the same moment Longstreet's infantry rushed like a tempest against Pope's left, driving everything before it. This assault was irresistible, and speedily decided the fortune of the day. Pope's left wing gave way before it at every point, and his right, being assailed in flank and threatened in rear, relaxed its efforts and began to retire.

The Confederates, seeing the enemy in re-treat, pursued with a shout that rose above the din of battle, and pressed him with such vigor that he soon fell into disorder and broke into rapid flight toward Bull Run. The pursuit was continued until arrested by the cover of night. After the storm of battle the field presened a scene of dreadful carnage. Thirty thousand men *hors de combat*, wrecks of batteries and the mangled carcasses of horses, gave proof of the desperate character of the conflict. Pope left upon the field 15,000 killed, wounded, and prisoners, while his army was greatly reduced by stragglers, who, imbued with the sentiment, "He who fights and runs away will live to fight another day," sought refuge far beyond the range of battle. The Confederate loss was also heavy, the killed and wounded being numbered at between 7000 and 8000. Beside the heavy losses in *personnel* sustained by the Federals, a large amount of valuable property fell into the hands of the victor, the most important of which was twenty-five thousand stand of small-arms and twenty-three pieces of artillery; also a large amount of medical stores was subsequently taken at Centreville.

Pope retired to Centreville, where he was opportunely joined by Generals Sumner and Franklin with 25,000 fresh troops, upon which Pope endeavored to rally his army.

General Lee, being well aware that powerful reinforcements from McClellan's and

BELOW: The dedication of a monument to the dead of First Bull Run in Virginia. Five times as many would die in the second campaign.

Burnside's armies and from other sources had been ordered to join Pope, did not deem it advisable to immediately pursue the retreating enemy, but prudently paused to ascertain what force he had to contend with before renewing the conflict. After the close of the battle Colonel Long made a personal reconnoissance of the whole field and reported to Lee. Wishing to strike the enemy another blow before he could recover from the effects of his repulse, Lee by rapid movement turned Centreville on the 1st of September, and took a position on the Little River turnpike, between Chantilly and Ox Hill, with the view of intercepting his retreat to Washington. This movement was covered by Robertson's cavalry, while Stuart advanced to Germantown, a small village a few miles east of Ox Hill, where he discovered the Federal army in retreat.

After a sharp attack Stuart was obliged to retire before a superior force. About dusk A. P. Hill's division encountered a large detachment of the enemy at Ox Hill. A brief but sanguinary combat ensued, ... The combatants being separated by night and storm, Hill's division occupied the field, while the Federals resumed the retreat. In this engagement they numbered among their slain two distinguished officers (Generals Kearny and Stephens), whose loss was regretted by friends in both armies. Pope made good his retreat during the night, and we once more see the fugitives from Manassas seeking a refuge within the defences of Washington.

*   *   *

43

Chapter III

Antietam

With the view of shedding additional light on this period of the history of the war, we shall here introduce a scrap of personal information. On the 2d of September succeeding Pope's defeat, Colonel Long wrote from the dictation of General Lee to President Davis in substance as follows: As Virginia was free from invaders, the Federal army being within the defences of Washington, shattered and dispirited by defeat, and as the passage of the Potomac could now be effected without opposition, the present was deemed a proper moment, with His Excellency's approbation, to penetrate into Maryland. The presence of the victorious army could not fail to alarm the Federal authorities and make them draw forces from every quarter for the defence of their capital, thus relieving the Confederacy from pressure and – for a time, at least – from the exhaustion incident to invasion. The presence of a powerful army would also revive the hopes of the Marylanders, allow them a free exercise of their sympathies, and give them an opportunity of rallying to the aid of their Southern friends. Above all, the position of the army, should it again be crowned with victory, would be most favorable for seizing and making the best use of the advantages which

such an event would produce. In conclusion, a few remarks were made in regard to the condition of the army.

In anticipation of the President's concurrence, General Lee immediately began the preparation for the invasion of Maryland. On the 3d he put the army in motion, and on the 4th took a position between Leesburg and the contiguous fords of the Potomac. The inhabitants of this section of country, having been crushed by the heel of oppression, were now transported with the cheering prospect of liberty. The presence of the army whose movements they had anxiously and proudly watched filled them with unbounded joy. Their doors were thrown open and their stores were spread out in hospitable profusion to welcome their honored guest. Leesburg, being on the border, had at an early period fallen into the hands of the enemy. All of the men who were able had joined the army, and many of those who were unfit for service had retired within the Confederate lines to escape the miseries of the Northern prison; so that the women and children had been left almost alone. Now all these gladly returned to their homes, and tender greetings on every side penetrated to the deepest recesses of the heart and made them thank God that misery and woe had

BELOW: Residents of Sharpsburg, Maryland, flee the town at the approach of Confederate troops.

been replaced by happiness and joy.

The strength of the Confederate army at this time, including D. H. Hill's division, did not exceed 45,000 effective men; yet, though it had been greatly reduced in numbers during the campaign through which it had just passed, its spirit was raised by the victories it had achieved. Its numerical diminution was not so much the result of casualties in battle as that of losses incident to long and rapid marches with insufficient supplies of food and the want of shoes. It frequently happened that the only food of the soldiers was the green corn and fruit gathered from the fields and orchards adjacent to the line of march, and often the bravest men were seen with lacerated feet painfully striving to keep pace with their comrades, until, worn out with pain and fatigue, they were obliged to yield and wait to be taken up by the ambulances or wagons, to be carried where their wants could be supplied.

The invasion of Maryland being determined on, the army was stripped of all incumbrances, and, from fear that the soldiers might be induced to retaliate on the defenceless inhabitants for outrages committed by the Federal troops upon the people of the South, stringent orders were issued against straggling and plundering. These orders were strictly enforced throughout the campaign.

* * *

The passage of the Potomac was successfully accomplished on the 5th. The infantry, artillery, and trains crossed at White's and Cheek's fords, the cavalry having previously crossed with instructions to seize important points and cover the movements of the army. From the Potomac, General Lee advanced to Frederick, at which place he arrived on the 6th and established himself behind the Monocacy. He at the same time seized the Baltimore and Ohio Railroad, and the principal roads to Baltimore, Washington, Harper's Ferry, and the upper Potomac. From this important position radiated several lines upon which he could operate. Those toward Harper's Ferry, Baltimore, and

ABOVE: A military wagon train crosses a river on a pontoon bridge.

ABOVE: Stonewall Jackson's men wading across the Potomac at White's Ford.

Pennsylvania were unoccupied, while that in the direction of Washington was held by the Federal army.

* * *

It was not without surprise that General Lee discovered, upon reaching Frederick, that Harper's Ferry was still garrisoned. He had expected on entering Maryland that it would be at once abandoned, as it should have been had ordinary military principles been observed. Its continued occupation subjected its defenders to imminent danger of capture. Yet, through a military error, its occupation was unfavorable to the success of the Confederate movement, particularly if there was any idea entertained by General Lee of invading Pennsylvania. It would not do to leave this strongly-fortified post, on the direct line of communication of the army, in possession of the enemy; yet to reduce it needed a separation and retardation of the army that seriously interfered with the projected movements, and might have resulted adversely to the Southern cause but for the rapidity of Jackson's marches and the errors

of Colonel Miles, the commander of the garrison. This will appear when we come to describe the subsequent events.

Yet, whatever might be the effect, its reduction was absolutely necessary where any further operations of importance could be undertaken. Nor could the whole army be judiciously used for this purpose. Not only is it extremely unusual for a commander to use his whole force for a service which can be performed by a detachment, but in this case it would have necessitated a recrossing of the Potomac, with the strong probability that McClellan would take sure measures to prevent a return of the army into Maryland.

This service, had the claims of senior rank been alone considered, should have been intrusted to Longstreet; but it was given to Jackson on account of his superior qualifications for duty of this character, Longstreet making no objection. Jackson was therefore directed to move his corps on the morning of the 10th by way of Williamsport to Martinsburg, to capture or disperse the Federal force at that place, and then proceed to Harper's Ferry and take steps for its immediate reduction. At the same time, Major-general McLaws was ordered to move with his and Anderson's divisions by the most direct route upon Maryland Heights, to seize that important position and co-operate with Jackson in his attack on Harper's Ferry. Brigadier-general Walker was instructed to recross the Potomac with his division and occupy Loudoun Heights for the same purpose. The several movements were executed with wonderful celerity and precision.

Jackson on leaving Frederick marched with great rapidity by way of Middletown, Boonsboro', and Williamsport, near which latter place he forded the Potomac on the 11th and entered Virginia. Here he disposed his forces so as to prevent an escape of the garrison of Harper's Ferry in this direction and marched upon that place, the rear of which he reached on the 13th. On his approach General White evacuated Martinsburg and retired with its garrison to Harper's Ferry. On reaching Bolivar Heights, Jackson found that Walker was already the foot of Maryland Heights, the key to Harper's Ferry, since it is the loftiest of the three heights by which that place is surrounded, and is sufficiently near to reach it even by musketry. Harper's Ferry, in fact, is a mere trap for its garrison, since it lies open to cannonade

LEFT: Colonel Dixon S. Miles commanded Union forces in the defense of Harper's Ferry. He died during the surrender on September 14.

from the three heights named; so that the occupation of these renders it completely untenable.

Colonel Miles had posted a small force under Colonel Ford on Maryland Heights, retaining the bulk of his troops in Harper's

BELOW: Federal defenders on Maryland Heights, the point commanding Harper's Ferry. The position was abandoned quickly and reoccupied by Confederate troops on September 13.

Ferry. Instead of removing his whole command to the heights, which military prudence plainly dictated, and which his subordinates strongly recommended, he insisted upon a literal obedience to General Halleck's orders to hold Harper's Ferry to the last extremity. In fact, Maryland Heights was quickly abandoned altogether, Ford but feebly resisting McLaws and retiring before his advance, first spiking his guns and hurling them down the steep declivity. This retreat left Maryland Heights open to occupation by the assailing force, and it was not long ere McLaws had succeeded in dragging some guns to the summit of the rugged ridge and placing them in position to command the garrison below. Jackson and Walker were already in position, and, by the morning of the 14th, Harper's Ferry was completely invested. During the day the summits of the other hills were crowned with artillery, which was ready to open fire by dawn . . . .

There was never a more complete trap than that into which the doomed garrison had suffered itself to fall. Escape and resistance were alike impossible. Maryland Heights might easily have been held until McClellan came up had the whole garrison defended it, but its abandonment was a fatal movement. They lay at the bottom of a funnel-shaped opening commanded by a

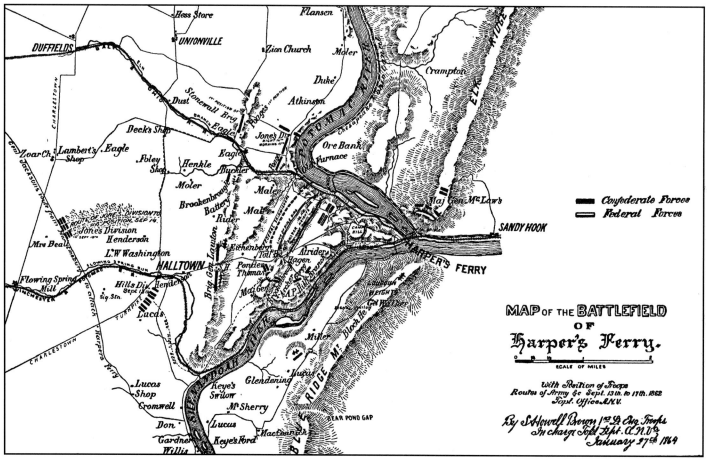

plunging fire from three directions and within reach of volleys of musketry from Maryland Heights. Two hours of cannonade sufficed to prove this, and at the end of that time Colonel Miles raised the white flag of surrender. The signal was not immediately perceived by the Confederates, who continued their fire, one of the shots killing the Federal commander. The force surrendered numbered between 11,000 and 12,000 men, while there fell into Jackson's hands 73 pieces of artillery, 13,000 stand of arms, 200 wagons, and a large quantity of military stores.

Pending the reduction of Harper's Ferry, General Lee moved by easy marches with two divisions of Longstreet's corps to the neighborhood of Hagerstown, leaving D. H. Hill with his division and a detachment of cavalry to serve as rear-guard, with instructions to hold the Boonsboro' pass of South Mountain. By taking a position between Williamsport and Hagerstown a junction could be easily effected with the troops operating against Harper's Ferry, and on the reduction of that place Lee would have a

secure line of communication through the Valley of Virginia, which would enable him to advance into Pennsylvania or to assume such other line of operation as circumstances might suggest.

Since the advance of the Confederate army into Maryland no considerable Federal force had appeared, and as yet only some unimportant cavalry affairs had occurred. After the evacuation of Virginia the Army of the Potomac had been augmented by the addition of the Army of Virginia and that of General Burnside, giving it an effective strength of about 90,000 men. This force was assigned to the command of General McClellan for active operations, and was put in motion about the 6th of September.

Although it was known in Washington that Lee had crossed the Potomac, McClellan was checked in his movements by General Halleck, who was still apprehensive that the ubiquitous Jackson or Stuart might suddenly appear before Washington.

When it became known that Lee had left Frederick and was advancing toward Hagerstown, McClellan advanced with greater

ABOVE: Union Major General Ambrose E. Burnside added his forces to McClellan's after the Federals evacuated Virginia.

OPPOSITE TOP: Union General-in-Chief Henry Halleck. His conflicting instructions to McClellan helped to slow the Union pursuit of Lee.

OPPOSITE BOTTOM: Map of troop positions and routes in the area of Harper's Ferry for the period from September 13 to 17.

confidence, and an attempt was made to relieve Harper's Ferry. Franklin was sent to force his way through Crampton's Pass, in the South Mountain range. This pass was defended by Mumford's cavalry, supported by a part of McLaws's division, under General Cobb, who had been sent back with three brigades under orders to hold Crampton's Pass until Harper's Ferry had surrendered, "even if he lost his last man in doing it." This pass is in the rear of, and but five miles from, Maryland Heights, and its occupation by the Federals would have seriously imperilled the Confederate operations. It was gallantly defended against the strong force of assailants, and, though Franklin succeeded in forcing his way through by the morning of the 15th, he was too late: Miles was already on the point of surrender. McLaws at once withdrew his force from Maryland Heights, with the exception of one regiment, and formed a line of battle across Pleasant Valley to resist the threatening corps. The surrender of the garrison immediately afterward left him a free line of retreat. He crossed the Potomac at the Ferry, and moved by way of Shepherdstown to rejoin Lee at Sharpsburg. The Confederates had in this enterprise met with the most complete and gratifying success.

The Federal army, moving with great caution and deliberation, reached Frederick on the 12th. Here occurred one of those un-

toward events which have so often changed the course of wars, and which in this instance completely modified the character of the campaign. A copy of General Lee's order directing the movements of the army accidentally fell into the hands of McClellan, who, being thus accurately informed of the position of the forces of his opponent, at once determined to abandon his cautious policy and boldly assume the offensive. He therefore pressed forward with the view of forcing the South Mountain passes, held by Hill, and of intruding himself between the wings of the Confederate army, with the hope of being able to crush them in detail before they could reunite.

The order in question, addressed to D. H. Hill, was found by a soldier after the Confederate evacuation of Frederick, and was quickly in McClellan's possession. Hill has been blamed for unpardonable carelessness in losing it; yet, as the original order was still in his possession after the war, it is evident that the one found must have been a copy. The mystery is made clear by Colonel Venable, one of General Lee's staff-officers, in the following remark: "This is very easily explained. One copy was sent directly to Hill from headquarters. General Jackson sent him a copy, as he regarded Hill in his command. It is Jackson's copy, in his own handwriting, which General Hill has. The other was undoubtedly left carelessly by some one at Hill's headquarters." However that be, its possession by McClellan immediately reversed the character of his movements, which were changed from snail-like slowness to energetic rapidity. In his own words, "Upon learning the contents of this order, I at once gave orders for a vigorous pursuit."

The detachment by General Lee of a large portion of his army for the reduction of Harper's Ferry was made with the reasonable assurance that that object could be effected and a junction formed before General McClellan would be in position to press him. Though this expectation proved well based, yet it was imperilled by the unforeseen event above mentioned.

The rapid movements to which the finding of Lee's order gave rise brought the leading corps of the Federal army in front of Hill's position upon South Mountain on the afternoon of the 13th. This mountain is intersected by three passes in front of Boonsboro'. The main, or central, pass is traversed by the Frederick and Boonsboro' turnpike; the second, three-fourths of a mile south-

BELOW: Confederate Brigadier General Howell Cobb of Georgia successfully defended a pass to Maryland Heights until the surrender of Harper's Ferry.

east of the first, is crossed by the old Sharpsburg turnpike; the third is an obscure pass behind the elevated crest, about a quarter of a mile north-west of the turnpike.

General Hill's right occupied the south-east pass, and his left held the central. The centre was posted on a narrow mountain-road connecting the right and left. The pass on the left was watched by a small cavalry force. The position of Hill was strong, as it was only assailable by the pike on the left and the road on the right and along the rugged mountain-sides.

Early on the morning of the 14th, General McClellan advanced to the attack, directing his principal efforts against the south-east pass. Hill maintained his position with his usual firmness and intrepidity, and his troops exhibited the same gallantry that had characterized them on various fields.

At this time the position of the several corps of the Confederate army was the following: Jackson was at Harper's Ferry, about fifteen miles from Sharpsburg; Longstreet, at Hagerstown, a somewhat greater distance to the north of Sharpsburg; and D. H. Hill, at Boonsboro' Gap, eastward of these positions; while McClellan's whole force, with the exception of the detachment sent toward Harper's Ferry, lay east of the Gap. Had the Gap been left undefended, as it has been recently suggested it should have been, there would have been nothing to hinder McClellan from inserting his army between the two sections of the Confederate forces and attacking them in detail. The occupation of Sharpsburg by the enemy would have placed Lee in a difficult and dangerous position. Had he retired across the Potomac, as it has been suggested was

ABOVE: General McClellan's headquarters guard, the New York 93rd Volunteers, gathers at Antietam for a photograph by Alexander Gardner, one of photographer Mathew B. Brady's staff, on September 16, 1862.

his proper course to pursue, it would have been a virtual abandonment of his trains and artillery, which were then extended along the road between Hagerstown and Sharpsburg, and could have been reached by McClellan with his cavalry in an hour or two from Boonsboro'.

The battle of Boonsboro' was therefore necessary to the security of the army; and when, on the night of the 13th, Lee received information of the rapid advance of McClellan, he at once took steps for the effective reinforcement of General Hill. Longstreet's corps was put in motion for this purpose early in the morning of the 14th, and, fortunately, arrived at the Gap in time to prevent Hill's brave men from being overwhelmed by the superior numbers of the enemy.

This timely reinforcement secured the Confederate position. McClellan, finding that his efforts against the centre and right were unavailing, at length discontinued them, with the intention of renewing the

conflict at a more assailable point. The contest during the morning had been severe and the loss on each side considerable. On the side of the Confederates, the chief loss fell on the brigade of Brigadier-general Garland. This brigade numbered among its slain its gallant commander, who fell while bravely opposing a fierce attack on South-east Pass.

When General Lee reached Boonsboro' with Longstreet's corps, he sent forward Colonel Long, Major Venable, and other members of his staff, to learn the condition of affairs in front. The pass on the left proved to be unoccupied, and a heavy Federal force was tending in that direction. In anticipation of an attack from this quarter, Hood's division was deployed across the turnpike and Rodes's was posted on the ridge overlooking the unoccupied pass, with Evans's brigade connecting his right with Hood's left. There was a small field in front of Evans and Hood, while Rodes was masked by the timber on the side of the mountain. About three

BELOW: Union scouts and guides for the Army for the Potomac photographed in October 1862 by Alexander Gardner.

o'clock the battle was renewed by McClellan, who with great energy directed his main attack against Rodes. This was successfully resisted until nightfall, when Rodes's troops gave way before the assault of a superior force. The possession of the ground that had been held by Rodes gave the Federals the command of the central pass, but they could not immediately avail themselves of their success, on account of the . . . darkness.

The Confederate position was now untenable, and its evacuation became necessary. The withdrawal of the rear-guard was assigned to General Rodes, the successful execution of the movement being in a great measure due to the sagacity and boldness of Major Green Peyton, adjutant-general of Rodes's division.

At ten o'clock the next morning the Confederate army was safely in position at Sharpsburg.

At Boonsboro', McClellan had displayed more than usual pertinacity in his attacks

LEFT: Confederate Major General James Longstreet opposed Lee's choice of Sharpsburg as the battle site. At the battle, his men formed Lee's right, anchored at Antietam Creek.

BELOW: The Boonesborough Pike crossing at Antietam Bridge in September 1862.

RIGHT: Map of battlefields at Antietam. At dawn on the 16th of September, some 40,000 of Lee's troops had been assembled against 90,000 of McClellan's.

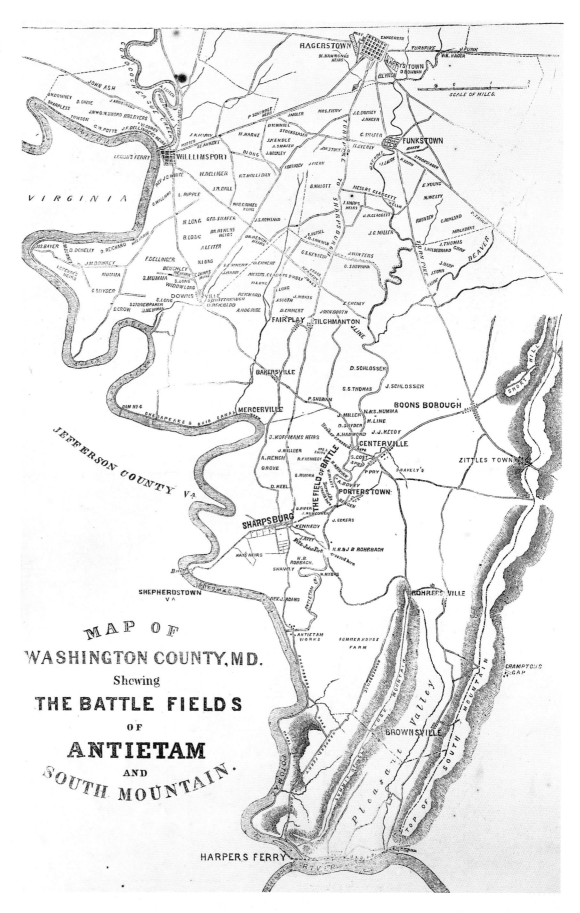

upon the Confederate position; yet these were met by the troops of Longstreet and Hill with a firmness worthy of the veterans of Manassas and the Chickahominy. Although Lee had been forced into an unexpected battle when his army was divided, he baffled McClellan in his designs by retarding him so as to gain time for the reduction of Harper's Ferry and to place himself where he could be easily joined by Jackson.

On the morning of the 15th, Harper's Ferry was surrendered, and about noon General

Lee received the report of its capture. Two courses now presented themselves to the general, each of which involved results of the highest importance. He might either retire across the Potomac and form a junction, in the neighborhood of Shepherdstown, with the forces that had been employed in the reduction of Harper's Ferry, or maintain his position at Sharpsburg and give battle to a superior force. By pursuing the former course the object of the campaign would be abandoned and the hope of co-operation from Maryland for ever relinquished. The latter, although hazardous, if successful would be productive of results more than commensurate with the risk attending its execution. Having a sympathy for the Marylanders, to whom he had offered his services, and a confidence in the bravery of his troops and the strength of his position, he adopted the latter course, and prepared to receive the attack of General McClellan.

Jackson's troops were hurried from Harper's Ferry and a strong defensive position was carefully selected. It embraced the heights fringing the right bank of the Antietam [the name by which the Battle of Sharpsburg is known in the North (Ed.)] east

and south-east of the village of Sharpsburg and a range of hills stretching north-west to the Potomac. Lee's right and centre were protected by stone fences and ledges of rock, and his left was principally covered by a wood. The right and centre were occupied by Longstreet's corps, D. H. Hill's division, and Lee's, Walton's, and Garnett's artillery, while Jackson's corps and Stuart's cavalry occupied the left. The Federal forces having been much shattered by the battle of the 14th, McClellan did not resume his advance until late on the morning of the 15th, and did not appear before Sharpsburg until afternoon.

He employed the following day chiefly in preparations for the battle. The corps of Hooker, Mansfield, Sumner, and Franklin, constituting his right, were massed opposite the Confederate left. The hills east of the Antietam which formed the centre of the Federal position were crowned by a powerful artillery, and Burnside's corps, which occupied the left, confronted the Confederate right. Porter's corps formed the reserve, while the cavalry operated on the flanks. Late in the afternoon Mansfield and Hooker crossed the Antietam opposite Longstreet's

BELOW: Currier & Ives print of the battle at Antietam Creek, the "bloodiest day of the war."

left. Some preliminary skirmishing closed the day. Both armies now lay on their arms, conscious that the next day would be marked by the most desperate battle that had yet been witnessed in the country. The Confederates, who had never known defeat, confident in themselves, confident in the strength of their position, and confident in their glorious leader, although less in numbers than their opponents by more than one-half, never doubted that victory would again rest on their tattered banners. The Federals, on their part, burning to obliterate the marks of defeat they had lately borne, were impatient for the approaching struggle. The Federal force present on the field amounted to 90,000 men; that of the Confederates, including the division of A. P. Hill, then at Harper's Ferry in charge of prisoners and captured property, amounted to 40,000.

At dawn on the 17th the corps of Mansfield and Hooker advanced to the attack; they were met by the divisions of Anderson and Hood with their usual vigor. Being greatly outnumbered, these divisions were reinforced by Evans's brigade and the division of D. H. Hill. The contest continued close and determined for more than an hour, when the Federals began to give way. They were hotly pressed. Hooker was wounded, Mansfield was killed, and their corps were irretrievably shattered when relieved by the fresh corps of Sumner and Franklin. The

Confederates, who had advanced more than a mile, were gradually borne back to their original position. McClellan now directed his chief attack upon Lee's left, with the hope of forcing it back, so that he might penetrate between it and the river and take the Confederate position in reverse. This attack was received by Jackson's corps with intrepidity. The veterans under Early, Trimble, Lawton, and Starke gallantly held their ground against large odds. At an opportune moment the Confederate line was reinforced by the division of McLaws and Walker. The entire Confederate force, except D. R. Jones's division, on the right, was now engaged.

The roar of musketry and the thunder of artillery proclaimed the deadly conflict that raged. These deafening sounds of battle continued until about twelve o'clock, when they began to abate, and about one they ceased. The Federals had been repulsed at every point, and four corps were so much broken by loss and fatigue that they were unable to renew the contest.

After the battle had concluded on the left General Burnside prepared to assault the Confederate right with 20,000 fresh troops. He had remained inactive during the forenoon; but when the attack on the Confederate left had failed, he proceeded to force the passage of the Antietam at the bridge southeast of Sharpsburg, on the Pleasant Valley

OPPOSITE TOP: Antietam Bridge after the battles.

OPPOSITE BOTTOM: Dead bodies of Confederates from North Carolina in the "Bloody Lane," scene of heavy fighting during the Battle of Antietam.

BELOW: Photograph by Alexander Gardner at Antietam. Long believed to be the only photo of battle action made during the war, it is actually a view of reserve artillery near Union headquarters on the day after the fighting.

road, and at the ford below. These points were gallantly maintained by Toombs's brigade of Jones's division until about four o'clock, when they were carried. General Burnside then crossed the Antietam and formed his troops under the bluff.

At five o'clock he advanced, and, quickly dispersing the small division of D. R. Jones, gained the crest of the ridge south of the town. At that moment the division of A. P. Hill, 4500 strong, just arrived from Harper's Ferry, was on the road which traverses its western slope. Seeing the Federal line on its flank, the division faced to the right, and, taking advantage of the stone fence that bordered the road, delivered such destructive volleys that the Federals were forced to retire as suddenly as they had appeared. Sharply followed by Hill and raked by the artillery, Burnside was forced to recross the Antietam. Just as the sun disappeared in the west the last of Burnside's corps gained the eastern side. Thus closed the battle of Sharpsburg. The Federal troops fought well and did honor to their gallant leaders, but, being compelled to attack a strong position defended by men who had been justly characterized as the finest soldiers of the

age, they failed to obtain the mastery of the field. The casualties on both sides were heavy; the numbers have never been accurately stated. On the side of the Federals were Mansfield killed, Major-general Hooker wounded, and a number of other distinguished officers killed or wounded; on the side of the Confederates, Brigadier-general Starke was killed and Brigadiers Lawton, Ripley, and G. B. Anderson were wounded, and a number of others were put *hors de combat*. Anderson afterward died of his wound.

Among the cases of individual gallantry, one of the most conspicuous was that of General Longstreet, with Majors Fairfax and Sorrell and Captain Latrobe of his staff, who, on observing a large Federal force approaching an unoccupied portion of his line, served with such effect two pieces of artillery that had been left without cannoneers that the Federals were arrested in their advance and speedily forced to retire beyond the range of the guns.

During the night General Lee prepared for the renewal of the battle the next day. A part of his line was withdrawn to the range of hills west of the town, which gave him a very

strong and much better field than that of the previous day. He remained in his new position during the 18th, prepared for battle; but General McClellan, perceiving that his troops had been greatly disorganized by the battle of the previous day, declined resuming the attack until the arrival of 15,000 fresh troops that were hastening to his support.

Foreseeing that no important results could be achieved by a second battle with McClellan's augmented forces, and being unwilling to sacrifice unnecessarily his gallant men, Lee withdrew during the night to the south side of the Potomac, and on the 19th took a position a few miles west of Shepherdstown.

When McClellan learned, on the morning of the 19th, that the Confederate position had been evacuated, he ordered an immediate pursuit, which, however, proved unavailing, as the Confederate rear-guard was disappearing in the defile leading from the ford below Shepherdstown when the Federal advance appeared on the opposite heights. A few batteries were then put into position, and a harmless cannonade commenced, which was kept up in a desultory manner during the greater part of the day. Late in the afternoon a large detachment approached the ford, and about nightfall dislodged General Pendleton, who had been charged with its defence, and effected a

BELOW: On October 4 President Lincoln went to the Antietam battlefield to try personally to persuade General McClellan to pursue General Lee. The Union general, however, would not cross the Potomac River into Virginia until October 26.

crossing without serious opposition. This occurrence was reported about midnight to General Lee, who immediately despatched orders to Jackson to take steps to arrest the Federal advance. The division of A. P. Hill, moving with rapidity, reached the mouth of the defile leading to the river just as the Federal detachment was debouching from it, and attacked this force with such impetuosity that it was compelled to retire with heavy loss across the Potomac. McClellan made no further attempt to continue offensive operations for several weeks, this interval being passed in the neighborhood of Sharpsburg in resting and reorganizing his forces. This campaign, especially the battle of Sharpsburg, has been the subject of much discussion, in which the Northern writers generally claim for the Federal arms a complete victory; but the historian of the Army of the Potomac, with greater impartiality, acknowledges Antietam (or Sharpsburg) to have been a drawn battle. This admission is corroborated by the evidence of General McClellan in his testimony before the Congressional Committee on the Conduct of the

War, since he admitted that his losses on the 17th had been so heavy, and that his forces were so greatly disorganized on the morning of the 18th, that, although General Lee still maintained a defiant attitude, he was unable to resume the attack. Swinton, however, claims for the Army of the Potomac a political victory, with apparent justice; but in reality his claim is without foundation, for Lee was politically defeated before the occurrence of a collision with McClellan by his failure to induce the Marylanders to rally in any considerable force to his standard; and even when McClellan, by accident, became aware of the disposition of his forces and his intentions, he was establishing a line of communication that would enable him to engage his opponent with no other hope of political results than such as would naturally arise from a victory, whether gained north or south of the Potomac. The severe chastisement that had been inflicted on the Army of the Potomac is evident from the long prostration it exhibited, notwithstanding the facility with which it received reinforcements and supplies.

ABOVE: Lincoln at Antietam with General McClellan. From left they are: Gen. G. W. Morell, Col. A. S. Webb, McClellan, scout Adams, Dr. J. Letterman, an unidentified officer, Lincoln, Col. H. J. Hunt, and Gen. Fitz John Porter.

Chapter IV

Fredericksburg.

After remaining a few days in the neighborhood of Shepherdstown, General Lee gradually withdrew to a position between Bunker Hill and Winchester. Notwithstanding he had failed, from accidental causes, to accomplish the chief object of the invasion of Maryland, the expedition was not wholly without beneficial results, since it relieved Virginia from the presence of the enemy and gave her an opportunity to recover in a measure from the exhausting effect of war . . . .

* * *

The inactivity of General McClellan allowed General Lee several weeks of uninterrupted repose. During that interval the guardianship of the Potomac was confided to the cavalry and horse-artillery. While thus employed General Stuart made a swoop into Pennsylvania, captured a thousand horses, and after making the entire circuit of the Federal army recrossed the Potomac with only the loss of three missing . . . .

Throughout the late campaign the duty of selecting a place for headquarters usually devolved upon the writer. The general would say, "Colonel Long has a good eye for locality: let him find a place for the camp." It was not always so easy to find a desirable situation, but, as the general was easily satisfied, the difficulties of the task were greatly lightened. Only once, to my recollection, did he object to the selection made for headquarters; this was on reaching the neighborhood of Winchester. The army had preceded the general and taken possession of every desirable camping-place. After a long and fatiguing search a farm-house was discovered, surrounded by a large shady yard. The occupants of the house with great satisfaction gave permission for the establishment of General Lee not only in the yard, but insisted on his occupying a part of the house. Everything being satisfactorily settled, the wagons were ordered up, but just as their unloading began the general rode up and flatly refused to occupy either

RIGHT: Lieutenant General Sir Garnet Wolseley, who, as Colonel, visited the Confederate camp near Winchester.

yard or house. No one expected him to violate his custom by occupying the house, but it was thought he would not object to a temporary occupation of the yard. Being vexed at having to look for another place for headquarters, I ordered the wagons into a field almost entirely covered with massive stones. The boulders were so large and thick that it was difficult to find space for the tents. The only redeeming feature the location possessed was a small stream of good water. When the tents were pitched, the general looked around with a smile of satisfaction, and said, "This is better than the yard. We will not now disturb those good people."

While occupying this camp we were visited by several distinguished British officers – among them, Colonel Garnet Wolseley, who has since become prominent in history. Subsequently, one of the number published the following account of General Lee and his surroundings:

In visiting the headquarters of the Confederate generals, but particularly those of General Lee, any one accustomed to see

European armies in the field, cannot fail to be struck with the great absence of all the pomp and circumstance of war in and around their encampments.

Lee's headquarters consisted of about seven or eight poletents, pitched, with their backs to a stake-fence, upon a piece of ground so rocky that it was unpleasant to ride over it, its only recommendation being a little stream of good water which flowed close by the general's tent. In front of the tents were some three or four army-wagons, drawn up without any regularity, and a number of horses turned loose about the field. The servants – who were, of course, slaves – and the mounted soldiers called couriers, who always accompany each general of division in the field, were unprovided with

tents, and slept in or under the wagons. Wagons, tents, and some of the horses were marked "U.S.," showing that part of that huge debt in the North has gone to furnishing even the Confederate generals with camp-equipments. No guard or sentries were to be seen in the vicinity, no crowd of aides-de-camp loitering about, making themselves agreeable to visitors and endeavoring to save their generals from receiving those who had no particular business. A large farm-house stands close by, which in any other army would have been the general's residence *pro tem.*; but, as no liberties are allowed to be taken with personal property in Lee's army, he is particular in setting a good example himself. His staff are crowded together, two or three in a

BELOW: A group of European officers who visited troops in the field near Yorktown, Va. in May 1862.

ABOVE: A Confederate camp in autumn.

RIGHT: Soldier drawing water for a hospital at Fredericksburg.

tent; none are allowed to carry more baggage than a small box each, and his own kit is but very little larger. Every one who approaches him does so with marked respect, although there is none of that bowing and flourishing of forage-caps which occurs in the presence of European generals; and, while all honor him and place implicit faith in his courage and ability, those with whom he is most intimate feel for him the affection of sons to a father. Old General Scott was correct in saying that when Lee joined the Southern cause it was worth as much as the accession of 20,000 men to the "rebels." Since then every injury that it was possible to inflict the Northerners have heaped upon him. Notwithstanding all these personal losses, however, when speaking of the Yankees he neither evinced any bitterness of feeling nor gave utterance to a single violent expression, but alluded to many of his former friends and companions among them in the kindest terms. He spoke as a man proud of the victories won by his country and confident of ultimate success

under the blessing of the Almighty, whom he glorified for past successes, and whose aid he invoked for all future operations.

Notwithstanding the ruggedness of this encampment, it proved unusually lively. Besides the foreign friends, we had numerous visitors from the army, also ladies and gentlemen from Winchester and the neighborhood, all of whom had some remark to make upon the rocky situation of our camp. This the general seemed to enjoy, as it gave him an opportunity of making a jest at the expense of Colonel Long, whom he accused of having set him down there among the rocks in revenge for his refusing to occupy the yard. Although there were no habitual drinkers on the general's staff, an occasional demijohn would find its way to headquarters. While at this place one of the officers received a present of a jug of fine old rye. Soon after its advent General J. E. B. Stuart, with Sweeney and his banjo, arrived – not on account, however, of the jug, but, as was his wont, to give us a serenade. The

ABOVE: Building a stockade at Alexandria, Virginia.

ABOVE: Night amusements around a Confederate campfire.

bright camp-fire was surrounded by a merry party, and a lively concert commenced. After a while the general came out, and, observing the jug perched on a boulder, asked with a merry smile, "Gentlemen, am I to thank General Stuart or the jug for this fine music?"

By this time the men had come to know their leader. The brilliant campaigns through which he had led them had inspired them with love and confidence, and whenever he appeared among them his approach was announced by "Here comes Mars' Robert!" and he would be immediately saluted with the well-known Confederate yell, which called forth in other quarters the exclamation, "There goes Mars' Robert – ole Jackson, or an ole hare."

* * *

The repose of a month had greatly improved in every way the Confederate army; it had reached a high state of efficiency, and General Lee was fully prepared to meet General McClellan whenever he might think fit to advance to attack him in his position

before Winchester. When McClellan . . . had crossed the Potomac and the direction of his advance was ascertained, Lee moved Longstreet's corps and the greater part of the cavalry to a position near Culpeper Courthouse and established his outposts along the right bank of the Rappahannock. Jackson's corps was detained in the Valley until the Federal plans should be more fully developed.

The delay that followed the battle of Sharpsburg and the deliberate manner in which McClellan resumed active operations . . . were productive of a voluminous correspondence with Mr. Lincoln and General Halleck, . . . which culminated in the removal of McClellan . . . .

* * *

A great diversity of opinion exists as to the military capacity of McClellan, and he has been both unduly praised and censured by his friends and foes. That his slowness and caution were elements on which the opposing general might safely count must be admitted, but that he had a high degree of

military ability cannot be denied. His skill in planning movements was certainly admirable, but their effect was in more than one instance lost by over-slowness in their execution. In this connection it will be of interest to give General Lee's own opinion concerning McClellan's ability, as related by a relative of the general, who had it from her father, an old gentleman of eighty years:

"One thing I remember hearing him say. He asked General Lee which in his opinion was the ablest of the Union generals; to which the latter answered, bringing his hand down on the table with an emphatic energy, 'McClellan, by all odds!'"

This opinion, however, could but have referred to his skill as a tactician, as it is unquestionable that Lee availed himself of McClellan's over-caution and essayed perilous movements which he could not have safely ventured in the presence of a more active opponent.

It was with surprise that the Confederate officers who knew the distinguished merit of Sumner, Sedgwick, Meade, and others learned that Burnside had been elevated

above them, and General Burnside himself with diffidence accepted the high honor that had been conferred upon him. Mr. Lincoln, accompanied by General Halleck, visited the headquarters of the army near Warrenton, where a plan of operations was adopted. A rapid advance upon Richmond by the way of Fredericksburg was advised. It was supposed from the position of General Lee's forces that by gaining a march or two upon him Richmond might be reached and captured before that general could relieve it. All that prevented the immediate execution of this plan was the want of a pontoon-train, which was necessary for the passage of the Rappahannock.

Having arranged to his satisfaction with General Halleck and Mr. Lincoln in regard to a prompt compliance with his requisitions for pontoons and supplies for the army, General Burnside, about the 15th of November, put the Army of the Potomac in motion, and on the 17th, Sumner's corps reached Fredericksburg. This energetic officer would probably have immediately crossed the Rappahannock by the fords above the town, and

ABOVE: Union General Meade (fourth from right) and General Sedgwick (second from right) were both considered more able than Major General Burnside, whom Lincoln chose to elevate over them as commander of the Army of the Potomac.

ABOVE: A Federal cavalry column forms up near a pontoon bridge after crossing the Rappahannock.

RIGHT: Federal earthworks on the north bank of the North Anna River facing Confederate earthworks in the distance.

OPPOSITE TOP: Three Confederate pickets at Fredericksburg.

OPPOSITE BOTTOM: Union pontoon wagons on the way to Burnside in December.

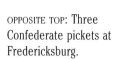

thus have saved much delay. He was, however, restrained by Burnside, who directed him to await the arrival of the pontoons. At this time the river in the neighborhood of Fredericksburg was held simply by a small picket-force, and could have been forded without much difficulty. General Lee, having penetrated the designs of the Federal commander, prepared to oppose them. About the 18th he sent reinforcements to Fredericksburg with instructions to retard, as far as practicable, the Federal forces in the passage of the Rappahannock, and at the same time he sent orders to Jackson to join him as speedily as possible.

Upon the supposition that Burnside would cross the Rappahannock before he could form a junction of his forces, Lee proposed to take a position behind the North Anna with part of Longstreet's corps, the force then about Richmond, and such other troops as might be drawn from other points, while, with Jackson's and the remainder of Longstreet's corps united, he moved in such a manner as might enable him to fall upon the flank and rear of the Federal army when it attempted the passage of that river. But when it was ascertained that Burnside was prevented from immediately crossing the Rappahannock by a delay in the arrival of his pontoons, Lee determined to move Longstreet's corps immediately to Fredericksburg and take possession of the heights opposite those occupied by the Federal force, as these heights afforded a stronger defensive line than the North Anna.

In execution of this determination Longstreet's corps left the vicinity of Culpeper Court-house on the 24th, crossed the Rapidan at Raccoon Ford, and, proceeding by the Wilderness road, reached Fredericksburg the next day. In the mean time, Jackson was rapidly approaching from the Valley. The Army of the Potomac had been a week before Fredericksburg and the pontoons had not yet arrived, and what might have been effected a few days before without opposition could now be accomplished only by force. Even after passing the river Burnside would be obliged to remove from his path a formidable opponent before he could continue his advance upon the city of Richmond.

On arriving at Fredericksburg, General Lee caused the heights south of the river to be occupied by artillery and infantry from Banks's Ford, four miles above, to the Massaponax, five miles below the city, while the

ABOVE: General Lee fortified the heights above the city of Fredericksburg. Shown are the breastworks erected on Marye's Heights (Marye's Hill).

cavalry extended up the river beyond the United States Ford and down as far as Port Royal. The prominent points were crowned with artillery covered by epaulments, and in the intervals were constructed breastworks for the protection of infantry. The heights closely fringe the river from Banks's Ford to Falmouth; thence they recede, leaving a low ground, which gradually increases in width to about two miles; then the hills again abut upon the river a little below the mouth of the Massaponax, and, extending nearly parallel to that stream, abruptly terminate in broad, low grounds. These low grounds are traversed by the main road to Bowling Green and are intersected by several small streams. The most important of these is Deep Run, which empties into the Rappahannock a little more than a mile above the mouth of the Massaponax. That portion of the road embraced between Deep Run and the Massaponax is enclosed by embankments sufficiently high and thick to afford good covers for troops. We have here endeavored to describe some of the principal features of the Confederate position at Fred-

ericksburg, that the plan of battle may be more clearly understood.

Jackson's corps on its arrival at the end of November was posted a few miles south of the Massaponax, in the neighborhood of Guinea Station on the Richmond and Fredericksburg Railroad. From this position he could easily support Longstreet, or, in case Burnside attempted a passage of the Rappahannock between the Massaponax and Port Royal, he would be ready to intercept him. After much delay the pontoon-train reached Fredericksburg. But then the position of Lee presented a formidable obstacle to the passage of the river at that point.

General Burnside thereupon caused careful reconnoissances to be made both above and below, with the view of finding a more favorable point for crossing. But he invariably found wherever he appeared the forces of General Lee ready to oppose him. Finding no part of the river more suitable or less guarded than that about Fredericksburg, Burnside determined to effect a crossing at that place. Two points were selected – one opposite the town, and the other two miles

Smoke from Battle field

ABOVE: A sketch by war artist Arthur Lumley shows some Union troops in Fredericksburg just before the start of the main battle. Lumley was criticized in the North for depicting the soldiers engaged in looting.

below, near the mouth of Deep Run – and early on the morning of the 11th of December the work was begun under cover of a dense fog. A bridge was laid at the mouth of Deep Run, and Franklin's grand division passed over without opposition. In front of Fredericksburg, however, the case was different. The gallant Barksdale with his brigade of Mississippians, to whom the defence of the town had been assigned, repelled every attempt to construct the bridges until the afternoon, when the powerful artillery of the Federal army was massed and a cannonade from one hundred and eighty guns was opened upon the devoted town, under cover of which troops crossed in boats under the direction of General Hunt, chief of artillery. Then Barksdale, fighting, retired step by step until he gained the cover of the road embankment at the foot of Marye's Heights, which he held until relieved by fresh troops. Burnside having developed his plan of attack, Lee concentrated his forces preparatory for battle. His right rested on the Massaponax, and his left on the Rappahannock at the dam in the vicinity

of Falmouth. Jackson's corps, in three lines, occupied the space between the Massaponax and Deep Run, while Longstreet's corps, with artillery, occupied the remainder of the position. The flanks were covered by Stuart's cavalry and horse artillery. It was here for the first time that the Confederate artillery was systematically massed for battle. On his arrival at Fredericksburg, General Lee assigned to Colonel Long the duty of verifying and selecting positions for the artillery, in which he was assisted by Majors Venable and Talcott and Captain Sam Johnson. On the day of battle two hundred pieces of artillery were in position, and so arranged that at least fifty pieces could be brought to bear on any threatened point, and on Fredericksburg and Deep Run, the points of attack, a hundred guns could be concentrated. The artillery on Longstreet's front was commanded by Colonels Alexander, Walton, and Cabell, and that on Jackson's by Colonels Brown and Walker. The horse artillery was commanded by Major Pelham. These officers on all occasions served with marked ability. General Pendleton, chief of artillery, exercised special control of the reserve artillery.

As Jackson's corps had been extended some distance down the Rappahannock, it was not until the night of the 11th that its concentration was completed. On the morning of the 12th of December, General Lee's entire force was in position, prepared to receive the Federal attack. The strength of the opposing armies, as on previous occasions, was disproportionate. The effective strength of the Army of Northern Virginia was about 60,000, of which about 52,000 were infantry, 4000 artillery with 250 guns, and the cavalry composed the remainder. That of the Army of the Potomac exceeded 100,000 men and 300 pieces of artillery. 90,000 men had crossed the river – 40,000 of Sumner's grand division at Fredericksburg, and Franklin's grand division of 50,000 men at Deep Run. From this disposition of forces it was ap-

parent that General Burnside designed a simultaneous attack upon the Confederate right and centre. Jackson's first line, composed of two brigades of A. P. Hill's division, held the railroad; a second line, consisting of artillery and the other brigades of Hill's division, occupied the heights immediately overlooking the railroad; and the reserves, commanded by D. H. Hill, were in convenient supporting-distance. In the centre the most conspicuous feature was Marye's Heights, behind the town of Fredericksburg and separated from it by an open space of several hundreds yards in width. The telegraph road passing between the base of the heights and a strong embankment was occupied by two brigades – Cobb's and Kershaw's of Longstreet's corps – while the crest was crowned by a powerful artillery covered by a continuous line of earthworks. A reserve of two brigades, commanded by

BELOW: Plan of the Battle of Fredericksburg, beginning on December 13, 1862. About 60,000 Confederates faced some 100,000 Federal troops.

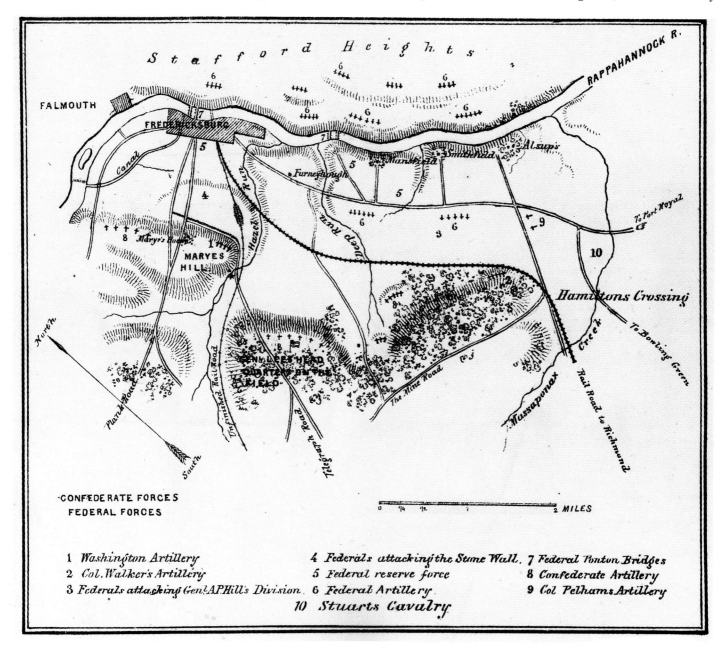

CONFEDERATE FORCES
FEDERAL FORCES

1 Washington Artillery
2 Col. Walker's Artillery
3 Federals attacking Gen! A.P.Hill's Division
4 Federals attacking the Stone Wall.
5 Federal reserve force
6 Federal Artillery
7 Federal Ponton Bridges
8 Confederate Artillery
9 Col. Pelham's Artillery
10 Stuarts Cavalry

LEFT: The opening bombardment by Union artillery positioned on Stafford Heights announced the start of the battle.

Brigadier-general Ransom, occupied the reverse slope of the heights. [These troops did good service during the battle.] On the hills behind were grouped batteries so disposed that the heights in front could be raked with shot and shell in case they were carried by the Federals.

On the morning of the 13th of December, as the fog slowly lifted, a scene was unfolded which in point of grandeur has seldom been witnessed. The Stafford Heights, from Falmouth to the Massaponax, were crowned with thickly-grouped batteries of artillery, while the shores of the Rappahannock were

BELOW: The Confederate defenders of Marye's Heights repulsed repeated Federal assaults.

ABOVE: Union artillery used to soften Confederate resistance at Fredericksburg.

covered with dark masses of troops in battle array. Opposite the Confederate right the attacking force, in two lines, began to advance. Simultaneously the heights were wreathed in smoke and the thunder of artillery announced the commencement of battle. When the attacking column had become disengaged from the embankments of the river-road, Stuart's horse artillery on the right and the artillery of Jackson's corps in front opened a destructive fire, which checked it for a brief space, until its own batteries could be placed in position to occupy the opposing artillery. It then moved steadily onward, and quickly dislodged the first Confederate line from the railroad, and disappeared in the wood that concealed the greater part of the second line. A deadly conflict ensued, which, although hidden by the forest, was proclaimed by the terrific clash of musketry. Very soon the troops that had advanced so gallantly were seen to retire. At first a straggling few and then large masses came rushing out, followed by long lines of gray veterans, who dealt death at every step.

General Meade, from the want of support after his gallant achievement, was compelled to witness the present deplorable condition of his corps. Forty thousand of Franklin's grand division, remaining idly by, had beheld the defeat of their brave comrades without extending a helping hand. This apathy of Franklin was at the time regarded by the Confederates as remarkable.

During the attack on the right preparations were in progress to assail the Confederate centre. Dense masses of troops, which had been previously concentrated in and about Fredericksburg, were now formed in columns of attack to be led against Marye's Heights. About noon the attack commenced. Column after column advanced to the assault, to be hurled back with terrible slaughter. Attack after attack was hopelessly renewed until the stoutest heart quailed at the dreadful carnage that ensued. Seeing his repeated efforts unavailing, General Burnside ordered a discontinuance of the conflict. The Confederates on the next day expected the battle to be renewed with greater vigor than had been displayed on the day before, but the Federals maintained a sullen silence, and at night recrossed the Rappahannock. The next morning the spectator could hardly believe his senses on beholding the great Federal army that had on the day previous lined the southern shore of the Rappahannock now covering the heights of Stafford, bereft of that martial spirit it had exhibited a few days before. The dispirited condition of the Federal army was not so much the consequence of losses in battle as the effect of the want of co-operation and the fruitless results of misdirected valor.

The appointment of General Burnside to the command of the Army of the Potomac had proved a mistake – more, however, from the combination of circumstances against him than from lack of conduct on his part. His successes in North Carolina had given him prominence, while his soldierly bearing and fine appearance evidently had their influence with Mr. Lincoln in the selection of him as commander-in-chief of the Army of the Potomac, while neglecting the superior claims of several others, two of whom – Generals Hooker and Franklin – could never forget their sense of superiority sufficiently to render him cordial co-operation. Bour-

BELOW: War artist A. R. Waud's on-the-scene sketch of Union soldiers building the pontoon bridge of the Rappahannock to attack Fredericksburg.

rienne gives us a maxim of Bonaparte that "two great generals in the same army are sure to make a bad one." This maxim particularly applied in the present instance to the Army of the Potomac, where its truth was fully verified.

The losses sustained, as stated by General Burnside, amounted to about 10,000, among whom was General Bayard, a young officer of great merit, whose loss was sincerely felt in the army as well as by a large circle of acquaintances. The Confederate loss was numerically much less than that sustained by the enemy. The Confederates, however, numbered among their slain Brigadier-generals Gregg and Cobb, and among their mortally wounded Colonel Coleman of the artillery. The fall of these noble and gallant spirits was deeply deplored by the army.

* * *

After the battle of Fredericksburg, General Lee retained his headquarters, established previous to the battle, at a point on the road midway between Fredericksburg and Hamilton Crossing, selected on account of its accessibility. Although there was a vacant house near which he could have occupied, he preferred ... to remain in camp, thus giving an example of endurance of hardship that might prove useful to his troops

* * *

OPPOSITE: Confederate dead behind the stone wall at the foot of Marye's Heights, from behind which Longstreet's infantry poured deadly fire on the Union attackers.

BELOW: Fredericksburg viewed from the river. Rebel troops stand on what remains of the town's wrecked bridge.

Chapter V

Chancellorsville.

The Army of Northern Virginia in the winter of 1862-63 began to feel seriously the want of . . . money and men. The Army of Northern Virginia was deficient in clothing, shoes, blankets, tents, provisions; in fact, everything needful was wanted except arms and ammunition . . . In order to relieve the drain upon the scanty commissariat, Longstreet was sent with two divisions to the district south of Petersburg, where provisions were still abundant, with a view of subsisting these troops, while they collected the surplus supplies to be sent to the troops in other quarters. This detachment reduced the Confederate army to barely 40,000 men, while the Federal force exceeded 100,000.

After this reduction General Lee conceived the design of adopting a position more remote from the Federal lines than the one he then occupied, . . . [but as] no position could be found which afforded greater advantages than the one he then occupied, Lee continued to hold the line of the Rappahannock, and busied himself in preparation for the ensuing campaign.

* * *

The appointment of Hooker to the command of the Army of the Potomac was a surprise to General Lee, who had no great respect for the military ability of his new opponent in a position of such importance. Swinton thus comments on the condition of the Army of the Potomac and the appointment of Hooker to the supreme command:

Notwithstanding the untoward fortunes the Army of the Potomac had suffered, it could hardly be said to be really demoralized, for

BELOW: By winter of 1862-63 the South began to grow short of materiel to support the war. Confederate soldiers are shown stripping clothing and boots from fallen Union soldiers.

its heart was still in the war; it never failed to respond to any demand made upon it; and it was ever ready to renew its courage at the first ray of hope. Such a day-spring came with the appointment of General Hooker to the chief command, and under his influence the tone of the army underwent a change that would appear astonishing had not its elastic vitality been so often proved. Hooker's measures of reform were judicious: he cut away the roots of many evils; stopped desertion and its causes; did away with the nuisance of the "grand-division" organization; infused vitality through the staff and administrative service; gave distinctive badges to the different corps; instituted a system of furloughs; consolidated the cavalry under able leaders, and soon enabled it not only to stand upon an equality with, but to assert its superiority over, the Virginia horsemen of Stuart. These things proved General Hooker to be an able administrative officer, but they did not prove him to be a competent commander for a great army, and whatever anticipation might be formed touching this had to be drawn from his previous career as a corps commander, in which he had won the reputation of being what is called a "dashing" officer, and carried the sobriquet of "Fighting Joe."

The new commander judiciously resolved to defer all grand military operations during the wet season, and the first three months after he assumed command were well spent in rehabilitating the army. The ranks were filled up by the return of absentees; the discipline and instruction of the troops were energetically continued; and the close of April found the Army of the Potomac in a high degree of efficiency in all arms. It numbered 120,000 men (infantry and artillery), with a body of 12,000 well-equipped cavalry and a powerful artillery force of above 400 guns. It was divided into seven corps – the First corps under General Reynolds; the Second under General Couch; the Third under General Sickles; the Fifth under General Meade; the Sixth under General Sedgwick; the Eleventh under General Howard; and the Twelfth under General Slocum.

During his period of preparation Hooker very properly resisted that spirit of impa-

ABOVE: Union General Joseph ("Fighting Joe") Hooker, who rehabilitated the Army of the Potomac in the winter 1862-63.

ABOVE: Company C of the 110th Pennsylvannia Infantry, part of Sickles's III Corps, on April 14, one week before it was cut to pieces at Chancerllorsville.

RIGHT: Hand-to-hand fighting between Union cavalry commanded by General William W. Averell and Confederates under Fitz Lee at Kelly's Ford on March 17.

tience that had characterized Mr. Lincoln in his intercourse with the previous commanders of the Army of the Potomac, and only gratified once that "up-and-be-doing" spirit that prevailed in Washington by indulging General Averill in a cavalry combat with General Fitz Lee, who guarded the upper fords of the Rappahannock. Being now fully prepared for active operations, Hooker determined to take the initiative by moving on the left of his opponent's position. By careful study of Lee's position he correctly concluded that his left was his most vulnerable point.

In order to mask his real design he sent forward a force of 10,000 cavalry under General Stoneman to operate upon Lee's lines of communication with Richmond, and sent Sedgwick with a force of 30,000 men still further to mask his movement. Stoneman crossed the Rappahannock at Kelly's Ford on the 29th, and Sedgwick appeared on the 28th on the heights below Fredericksburg. These preparatory measures having been taken, Hooker proceeded to the execution of his plan. Swinton, after a picturesque description of the passage of the Rappahannock and the Rapidan, tells us "that on the afternoon of the 30th of April four corps of the Federal army had gained the position of Chancellorsville, where Hooker at the same time established his headquarters."

Chancellorsville is situated ten miles south-west of Fredericksburg. It is not, as its name implies, a town or village, but simply a farm-house with its usual appendages, situated at the edge of a small field surrounded by a dense thicket of second growth, which sprang up after the primeval forest had been cut to furnish fuel to a neighboring furnace. This thicket extends for miles in every direction, and its wild aspect very properly suggests its name, The Wilderness. The intersection of several important roads gives it the semblance of strategic importance, while in reality a more unfavorable place for military operations could not well be found.

Hooker, however, seemed well pleased with his acquisition, for on reaching Chancellorsville on Thursday night he issued an order to the troops in which he announced that "the enemy must either ingloriously fly or come out from behind his defences and give us battle on our own ground, where certain destruction awaits him." This boast, we are told, so much in the style of Hooker, was amplified by the whole tenor of his conver-

Splendid advance of Sykes's Regulars.

Centre of our line of Battle

sation. "The Confederate army," said he, "is now the legitimate property of the Army of the Potomac. They may as well pack up their haversacks and make for Richmond, and I shall be after them," etc.

General Lee was fully aware of the preparations that were being made by his adversary, but calmly awaited the complete development of his plans before exerting his strength to oppose him. The presence of the enemy during the winter had made it necessary to maintain a defensive line of about twenty-five miles, the right being in the vicinity of Port Royal, while the left extended to the neighborhood of the United States Ford. This line was occupied by six divisions: Anderson's on the left, and McLaws's between Fredericksburg and the Massaponax,

ABOVE: Some sketches of the action at Chancellorsville by field artist A. R. Waud.

RIGHT: Confederate General Fitzhugh ("Fitz") Lee led one of Stuart's two cavalry units.

OPPOSITE BOTTOM: Union pontoon bridge across the Rappahannock.

BELOW: William Henry Fitzhugh Lee, the second of Robert E. Lee's three sons, commanded the second of Stuart's two cavalry brigades.

while the four divisions of Jackson's corps occupied the space below the Massaponax. This line had been greatly attenuated by the removal of Longstreet's two divisions of 15,000 men.

Lee's whole cavalry force consisted of two brigades – Fitz Lee's and W. H. F. Lee's – under the immediate command of Stuart, and was mainly employed in guarding the fords of the upper Rappahannock. Hooker had no sooner commenced his movement than it was reported by Stuart to General Lee, and Sedgwick's appearance on the 28th came under his own observation. Perceiving that the time for action had arrived, Lee ordered Jackson to concentrate his whole corps in the immediate vicinity of Fredericksburg.

Early on the morning of the 29th, Sedgwick crossed the Rappahannock below the mouth of Deep Run, but made no other aggressive movement on that day or the day following. On the night of the 30th, Lee was informed of Hooker's arrival at Chancellorsville. He had been previously informed of Stoneman's movements against his line of operations by General Stuart, and was now satisfied that the main attack of the enemy would come from the direction of Chancellorsville. Therefore on the morning of the 1st of May he made the necessary preparations to meet it. Accompanied by his staff, he took a position on a height where one of his batteries overlooked the Rappahannock. He there observed carefully the position of Sedgwick while waiting for information from the direction of Chancellorsville. Jackson was present, while his troops occupied the telegraph road. As far as the eye could reach these men with their bright muskets and tarnished uniforms were distributed in picturesque groups, lightly chatting and laughing, and awaiting the order to march.

Very soon the sound of cannon indicated that the work had begun. At the same time couriers arrived from Stuart and Anderson informing the general that the enemy were advancing on the old turnpike, the plank road, and on the river roads, and asking for reinforcements. McLaws was immediately ordered to the support of Anderson, and shortly after Jackson was ordered to follow with three of his divisions, leaving Early with his division, Barksdale's brigade, and the reserve artillery under General Pendleton – a force of about 9000 men and 45 pieces of artillery – in observation of Sedgwick. When Jackson joined McLaws and Anderson a lively skirmish was in progress, in which he immediately participated. When General Lee arrived he found the Federals were being driven back to Chancellorsville. At the close of the afternoon they had retired within their lines.

General Lee occupied the ridge about three-quarters of a mile south-east and south of Chancellorsville. The opposing armies were hidden from each other by the intervening thicket of brushwood. By a close examination it was discovered that the Federal position was protected by two strong lines of breastworks, one fronting east and the other south. The brushwood had been cleared off for a space of a hundred yards, thus giving an unobstructed field for musketry, while the roads were commanded by artillery. Toward the north and west the position was open. It was obvious that the Federal position was too formidable to be attacked in front with any hope of success; therefore Lee proceeded to devise a plan by which the position of Hooker might be turned and a point of attack gained from

which no danger was apprehended by the Federal commander.

General Lee was informed that the Rev. Mr. Lacy, a chaplain in Jackson's corps, was familiar with the country about Chancellorsville. Mr. Lacy informed the general that he

BELOW: A prayer in Stonewall Jackson's camp. The general stands at left, with A. P. Hill seated on his right and R. S. Ewell on his left.

OPPOSITE: A depiction of the last meeting between Robert E. Lee and Stonewall Jackson on the evening of May 1.

had been the pastor of a church near Chancellorsville, and was well acquainted with all the roads in that neighborhood, and that troops could be conducted to a designated point beyond Chancellorsville by a road sufficiently remote from the Federal position to prevent discovery. With this information Lee determined to turn the Federal position and assail it from a point where an attack was unexpected. The execution of a movement so much in accordance with his genius and inclination was assigned to General Jackson, Captain Carter acting as guide.

The above statement is made from personal knowledge of the writer, gained on the ground at the time; still, since some of Jackson's biographers have allowed their partiality for him so far to outstrip their knowledge of facts as to claim for him the origin of that movement, I will introduce, in corroboration of my statement, the following letter from General Lee published in the address of General Fitzhugh Lee before the Southern Historical Society:

LEXINGTON, VA., *October 28, 1867*
Dr. A. T. BLEDSOE, Office Southern Review, Baltimore, Maryland.

MY DEAR SIR: In reply to your inquiry, I must acknowledge that I have not read the article on Chancellorsville in the last number of the *Southern Review*, nor have I read

BELOW: Map of the positions of Union and Confederate forces at Chancellorville, May 1 to 5.

any of the books published on either side since the termination of hostilities. I have as yet felt no desire to revive any recollections of those events, and have been satisfied with the knowledge I possessed of what transpired. I have, however, learned from others that the various authors of the life of Jackson award to him the credit of the success gained by the Army of Northern Virginia when he was present, and describe the movements of his corps or command as independent of the general plan of operations and undertaken at his own suggestion and upon his own responsibility. I have the greatest reluctance to do anything that might be considered detracting from his well-deserved fame, for I believe no one was more convinced of his worth or appreciated him more highly than myself; yet your knowledge of military affairs, if you have none of the events themselves, will teach you that this could not have been so. Every movement of an army must be well considered and properly ordered, and every one who knew General Jackson must know that he was too good a soldier to violate this fundamental principle. In the operations around Chancellorsville I overtook General Jackson, who had been placed in command of the advance as the skirmishers of the approaching armies met, advanced with the troops to the Federal line of defences, and

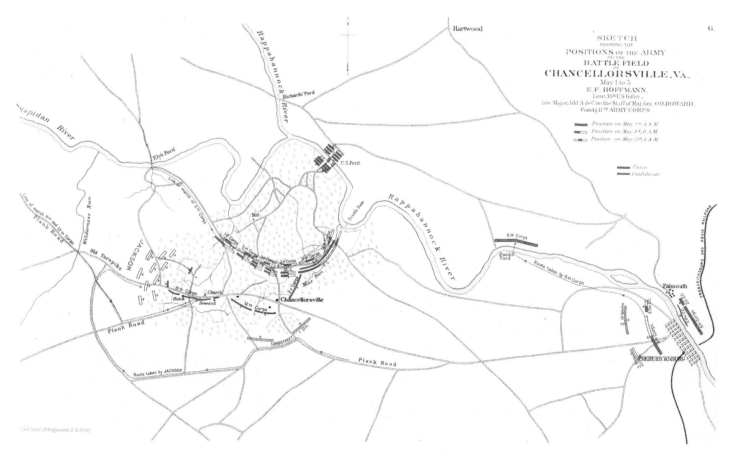

was on the field until their whole army re-crossed the Rappahannock. There is no question as to who was responsible for the operations of the Confederates, or to whom any failure would have been charged.

What I have said is for your own information. With my best wishes for the success of the *Southern Review* and for your own welfare, in both of which I take a lively interest,

I am, with great respect, your friend and servant,

R. E. LEE.

The last interview between Lee and Jackson, during which this important movement was decided upon, was an occasion of great historical interest, in regard to which the writer is fortunately able to add some information from his own knowledge of the circumstances, and that of other members of General Lee's staff. He has been favored by Major T. M. R. Talcott with certain important details of this event, conveyed in a private letter, from which the following extract is made:

My recollections of the night before the battle of Chancellorsville are briefly as follows:

About sunset General Jackson sent word to General Lee (by me) that his advance was checked and that the enemy was in force at Chancellorsville. This brought General Lee to the front, and General Jackson met him in the south-east angle of the Chancellorsville and Catharine Forge roads.

General Lee asked General Jackson whether he had ascertained the position and strength of the enemy on our left, to which General Jackson replied by stating the result of an attack made by Stuart's cavalry near Catharine Forge about dusk. The position of the enemy immediately in front was then discussed, and Captain Boswell and myself were sent to make a moonlight reconnoissance, the result of which was reported about 10 P.M., and was not favorable to an attack in front.

At this time Generals Lee and Jackson were together, and Lee, who had a map before him, asked Jackson, "How can we get at these people?" To which Jackson replied, in effect, "You know best. Show me what to do, and we will try to do it." General Lee looked thoughtfully at the map; then indicated on it and explained the movement he desired General Jackson to make, and closed by saying, "General Stuart will cover your movement with his cavalry." General Jackson listened attentively, and his face lighted up with a smile while General Lee was speaking. Then rising and touching his cap, he said, "My troops will move at four o'clock."

Having, in the manner here described, settled upon their plan of operations for the ensuing day, the two generals, accompanied by their staff officers, repaired to a neighboring pine-thicket, where an open space, well sheltered by overhanging boughs, afforded the party a good bivouac. The day having been a fatiguing one, they lost little time in preparing for the night's repose. Each selected his ground for a bed, spread his saddle-blanket, substituted his saddle for a pillow and his overcoat for covering, and was soon in a happy state of oblivion.

At dawn on the morning of the 2d, Jackson's corps, 22,000 strong, was in motion, and while it was making one of the most famous flank movements on record, General Lee, with the divisions of Anderson and McLaws, with 20 pieces of artillery, a force not exceeding 12,000 men, occupied the position he had assumed the previous evening, and General Hooker, with 90,000 men, lay behind his breastworks awaiting the Confederate attack. Having in the fore-

BELOW: Union Major General Daniel Sickles won several engagements on May 2 before the Federal defeat. (The photo was taken postwar.)

noon seen a part of Jackson's ammunition-train, Hooker believed that Lee was retreating, and sent two divisions of Sickles's corps and Pleasonton's cavalry to gain information. This movement was promptly arrested by Colonel Thompson Brown with his battalion of artillery, supported by Jackson's rearguard. Sickles's and Pleasonton's cavalry lingered about Catharine Furnace in a state of uncertainty until recalled by Jackson's attack on the right of the Federal position.

After making a circuitous march of fifteen miles, Jackson reached a point on the Orange Court-house road three miles in the rear of Chancellorsville. Had Hooker possessed a handful of cavalry equal in spirit to the "Virginia horsemen" under W. H. F. Lee that neutralized Stoneman's ten thousand, he might have escaped the peril that now awaited him. On the arrival of Jackson on the plank road, Fitz Lee, who had covered his movement with his brigade of cavalry, conducted him to a position from which he obtained a view of the enemy, which disclosed the following scene:

Below and but a few hundred yards distant ran the Federal line of battle. There was the line of defence, with abatis in front and long lines of stacked arms in rear. Two cannons were visible in the part of the line seen. The soldiers were in groups in the rear, laughing, chatting, and smoking, probably engaged here and there in games of cards and other amusements, indulged in while feeling safe and comfortable, awaiting orders. In the rear of them were other parties driving up and butchering beeves.

ABOVE: Union General Alfred Pleasonton's artillery attacking Jackon's men at Hazel Grove on May 3.

BELOW: Woodcut of a cavalry engagement at Chancellorsville.

OPPOSITE TOP: Jackson being cheered by his troops.

OPPOSITE BOTTOM: The wounding of General Stonewall Jackson on May 2.

BELOW: Sketches by A. R. Waud show an attack by Jackson on the Union Second and Third Corps and a view of General Hooker's field headquarters.

Returning from this point of observation, Jackson proceeded to make his dispositions of attack, which by six o'clock were completed. The divisions of Rodes and Colston were formed at right angles to the old turnpike, the division of Rodes being in advance, and the division of A. P. Hill, in column on the road, formed the reserve.

Howard's corps was first assailed. This corps, being surprised, was panic-stricken and fled precipitately, and in its flight communicated the panic to the troops through which it passed. Jackson's forces followed, routing line after line, until arrested by the close of day. The rout of the Federal army was fast becoming general, and it was only saved from entire defeat by the interposition of night. When compelled to halt Jackson remarked that with one more hour of daylight he could have completed the destruction of the Federal army.

This, the most famous of all Jackson's brilliant achievements, closed his military career. After his troops had halted, and while the lines were being adjusted, he rode forward with several of his staff to reconnoitre the Federal position. It was then after nine o'clock at night. The moon faintly illuminated the scene, but floating clouds dimmed its light. The battle had ceased, and

deep silence reigned over what recently had been the scene of war's fiercest turmoil. The reconnoitering party rode several hundred yards in advance of the lines, and halted to listen for any sounds that might come from the direction of the enemy, when suddenly a volley was poured into them from the right of the road. They had been mistaken for Federal scouts by the Confederate infantry. Some of the party fell, and Jackson wheeled his horse in the wood in dread of a renewal of the fire.

This movement proved an unfortunate one. It brought him directly in front of, and not twenty paces from, a portion of his own men, who had been warned against a possible attack from the Federal cavalry. A volley saluted him, with the unfortunate effect of wounding him in three places – two bullets striking his left arm, and one his right hand. At this moment his left hand held the bridle, while his right was held erect, perhaps to protect his face from boughs, yet seemingly with the peculiar gesture which he frequently used in battle. When the bullets struck him his wounded hand dropped, but he instantly seized the bridle with his bleeding right hand, while the frightened horse wheeled and darted through the wood. As he did so the limb of a pine tree

struck Jackson in the face, hurled off his cap, and nearly flung him to the ground. Retaining his seat with difficulty, he reached the road and his own lines, where he was assisted to dismount by Captain Wilbourn, one of his staff officers, who laid him at the foot of a tree.

He was soon afterward supported to the rear by his officers, and, becoming so weak as to be unable to walk, was placed in a litter and borne from the field. His last order, as he was being carried back, was given to General Pender, who had expressed doubts of being able to hold his position. The eyes of the wounded hero flashed as he energetically replied, "You *must* hold your ground, General Pender! You *must* hold your ground, sir!"

The discharge of musketry provoked a terrible response from the Federal batteries, which swept the ground as Jackson was being borne from the field. During this movement one of the bearers stumbled and let fall his end of the litter. A groan of agony came from the wounded man, and in the moonlight his face looked deathly pale. On being asked, however, if he was much hurt, he replied, "No, my friend; don't trouble yourself about me."

There is an incident of considerable interest in relation to the wounding of General Jackson which has never yet been told, yet is worthy of being put on record as one of those remarkable coincidences which have so often happened in the lives of great men. On the morning of May 2d, Jackson was the first to rise from the bivouac above described, and, observing a staff officer (General W. N. Pendleton) without cover, he spread over him his own overcoat. The morning being chilly, he drew near a small fire that had been kindled by a courier, and the writer, who soon after sought the same place, found him seated on a cracker-box. He complained of the cold, and, as the cooks were preparing breakfast, I managed to procure him a cup of hot coffee, which by good fortune our cook was able to provide.

While we were still talking the general's sword, which was leaning against a tree, without *apparent* cause fell with a clank to the ground. I picked it up and handed it to him. He thanked me and buckled it on. It was now about dawn, the troops were on the march, and our bivouac was all astir. After a few words with General Lee he mounted his horse and rode off. This was the last meeting of Lee and Jackson.

I have spoken of the falling of Jackson's sword because it strongly impressed me at the time as an omen of evil – an indefinable superstition such as sometimes affects persons on the falling of a picture or mirror. This feeling haunted me the whole day, and when the tidings of Jackson's wound reached my ears it was without surprise that I heard this unfortunate confirmation of the superstitious fears with which I had been so oppressed.

After the fall of Jackson the command fell to General Stuart, who was co-operating with him, and was the senior officer present, General A. P. Hill having been wounded at the same time with Jackson. About midnight Lee received from Stuart the report both of Jackson's wound and his success. Instructions were sent to Stuart to continue what had been so successfully begun, and Anderson was directed to support him, while McLaws threatened Hooker's right.

Early on the morning of the 3d the attack was resumed by the Confederates with great vigor. Hooker, taking advantage of the night, had restored order in his army and strengthened his position; his troops regained courage and contested the field with great stubbornness until ten o'clock, when they yielded at every point and rapidly retreated before the impetuous assaults of Rodes, Heth, Pender, Doles, Archer, and other gallant leaders within a strong line of defences

BELOW: The death of Stonewall Jackson. Wounded by the fire of a South Carolina regiment which had mistaken his escort for Federal cavalry, Jackson died on May 10 at Guinea's Station, Virginia. He was 39.

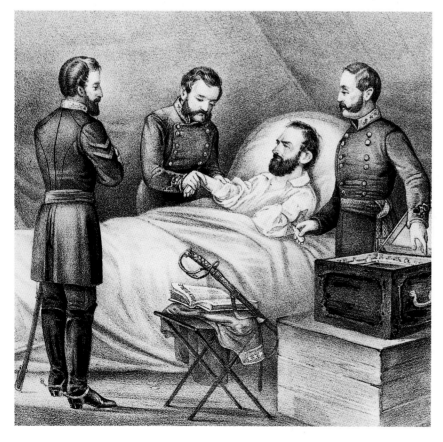

which had been previously constructed to cover the road to the United States Ford, their line of communication with the north side of the Rappahannock. When Stuart assumed the direction of affairs on the night of the 2d the command of the cavalry devolved on Fitz Lee, who operated with vigor on the flanks of the enemy during the continuance of the operations about Chancellorsville.

* * *

The troops being much fatigued and having accomplished all that could have been expected of them, Lee caused a suspension of further operations in order that they might rest and refresh themselves preparatory for the final blow. While the operations above described were in progress at Chancellorsville, General Early by skilful manoeuvring had detained Sedgwick at Fredericksburg until the 3d, when that general, by a determined advance, forced back Early, carried Marye's Heights, and proceeded toward Chancellorsville. The con-

dition of affairs was communicated to General Lee during the forenoon. Wilcox's brigade, then at Banks's Ford, was ordered to intercept Sedgwick and retard his advance, while McLaws's division was ordered to support him. Wilcox on reaching Salem Church, six miles from Chancellorsville, encountered the Federal advance, and after a sharp conflict he repulsed it with loss.

The success of Wilcox delayed Sedgwick until Anderson and McLaws could come up. The premeditated attack on Hooker being thus interrupted, Lee on the forenoon of the 4th repaired to the neighborhood of Fredericksburg. A combined attack was then directed to be made by Early on the rear, while McLaws and Anderson bore down upon the front. The battle was hotly contested during the afternoon, in which the forces of Sedgwick were defeated, and were only saved from destruction by a night-passage across the Rappahannock at Banks's Ford. On the 5th, Lee collected his forces at Chancellorsville to give the *coup de grâce* to Hooker, but that general, under cover of a

BELOW: In the aftermath of the Battle of Chancellorsville lie the remains of a Confederate caisson.

ABOVE: Removing Union dead from the battlefield.

dark and stormy night, effected his retreat beyond the Rappahannock at the United States Ford.

The losses sustained at Chancellorsville and Fredericksburg were estimated at the time at 20,000 killed and wounded, and among the wounded was General Hooker, besides a large number of prisoners. Swinton places Hooker's loss at Chancellorsville at 17,000; Sedgwick's loss at Fredericksburg must have considerably increased that number. The loss sustained by the Confederates was proportionately as great as that of the Federals. The casualties reported were about 9000. After expressing his praise and admiration for the heroic conduct of his troops, and after mentioning the names of a large number of line officers whose zeal and gallantry entitled them to special notice, General Lee thus concludes his report:

The loss of the enemy in the battle of Chancellorsville and the other engagements was severe. His dead and a large number of wounded were left on the field. About 5000 prisoners exclusive of the wounded were taken, and 13 pieces of artillery, 19,500 stands of arms, 17 colors, and a large quantity of ammunition fell into our hands. To the members of my staff I am greatly indebted for assistance in observing the movements of the enemy, posting troops, and conveying orders. On so extended and varied a field all were called into requisition and all evinced the greatest energy and zeal. The medical director of the army, Surgeon Guild, with the officers of his department, were untiring in their attention to the wounded. Lieutenant-colonel Corley, chief quartermaster, took charge of the disposition and safety of the trains of the army. Lieutenant-colonel Cole, chief commissary of subsistence, and Lieutenant-colonel Baldwin, chief of ordnance, were everywhere on the field attending to the wants of their departments; General Chilton, chief of staff, Lieutenant-colonel Murray, Major Peyton, and Captain Young, of the adjutant- and inspector-general's department, were active in seeing to the execution of orders; Lieutenant-colonel Proctor Smith and Captain Johnston of the Engineers in reconnoitering the enemy and constructing batteries; Colonel Long in posting troops and artillery; Majors Taylor, Talcott, Marshall, and Venable were engaged night and day in watching the operations, carrying orders, etc.

Respectfully submitted,
R. E. LEE, General.

NOTE. – Notwithstanding the unfavorable character of the country for the use of artillery, Colonels Brown, Carter, and Hardaway succeeded in placing thirty or forty guns in position to be used with effect on parts of the enemy's position, especially that in the vicinity of the Chancellor house.

On the 7th, General Lee ordered his troops to resume their former position about Fredericksburg. A few days after the sad intelligence of the death of Lieutenant-general Jackson reached the army. The estimation in which that distinguished officer was held will be best explained by the general orders of the commander-in-chief announcing his death to the army:

HEADQUARTERS ARMY OF NORTHERN VIRGINIA, MAY 11, 1863

General Orders No. 61.

With deep regret the commanding general announces to the army the death of Lieutenant-general T. J. Jackson, who expired on the 10th instant at a quarter past 3 P.M. The daring, skill, and energy of this great and good soldier by the decree of an all-wise Providence are now lost us. But while we mourn his death we feel that his spirit still lives, and will inspire the whole army with his indomitable courage and unshaken confidence in God as our hope and strength. Let his name be a watchword to his corps, who have followed him to victory on so many fields. Let his officers and soldiers emulate his invincible determination to do everything in the defence of our beloved country.

R. E. LEE, General.

It is but just to pause at this point in our narrative, and append some remarks upon the appearance and character of this remarkable man. . . .

The writer first knew Jackson as a young man, then an officer in the First Artillery. Shortly after that time he retired from the army and became a professor in the Virginia Military Institute, which he left to join the army of the Confederacy. I next saw him in Richmond when on a brief visit to Lee to consult in regard to the projected movement against McClellan. He seemed then in much better health than before he left the United States army, but presented the same tall,

ABOVE: Cover of a song sheet dedicated to Jackson after his death.

BELOW: Burying the dead at a hospital in Fredericksburg. Casualties on both sides were great, but the Confederates once again saw the Army of the Potomac withdraw across the Rappahannock.

gaunt, awkward figure and the rusty gray dress and still rustier gray forage-cap by which he was distinguished from the spruce young officers under him. There was nothing of a very striking character in his personal appearance. He had a good face, but one that promised no unusual powers. Yet in the excitement of battle his countenance would light up and his form appear to expand, a peculiar animation seeming to infuse itself through his whole person. At the battle of Gaines's Mill, where I next saw him, he was very poorly mounted on an old sorrel horse, and in his rusty suit was anything but a striking figure. And yet as he put himself at the head of his last regiment and advanced with his face lit up with the enthusiasm of war, he looked truly heroic and appeared a man made by Nature to lead armies to victory.

I saw him frequently afterward during the progress of the war, and in the march against Harper's Ferry I wrote off the order for the movement. The conversation in regard to it between Lee and Jackson took

BELOW: Engraving of Stonewall Jackson from an original field sketch.

place in my presence, and I well remember not only his strong approval of it, but also the earnest energy with which he undertook the enterprise. He at that time seemed improved in health, and was more animated than usual in manner. It was in the camp near Winchester, however, that Jackson presented his most attractive appearance. General Stuart had made him a present of a new uniform, and a handsome horse in place of his old raw-boned sorrel. It was with some difficulty that he was induced to part with his ancient attire in favor of this new and showy dress, and it is doubtful if he was ever quite comfortable in it.

He was a very reticent man, and ordinarily seemed absorbed in his own thoughts, while he displayed some marked peculiarities of manner. One of these was a strange habit of stopping and throwing up his hands, as if in supplication to the Invisible. In religion he was a strict Presbyterian of the sternest creed, and very attentive to religious observances. He not only believed in predestination, but had a strong belief in his personal safety – a presentiment that he would never fall by the hands of the enemy that seemed singularly warranted by the result. The men under his command were to a considerable extent of his own faith. In this he presented a parallel with Cromwell, whom, indeed, he resembled in character.

Jackson was very hospitable in disposition and welcomed warmly any guest to his tent or his table. The writer has often partaken of his hospitality, and found him ever an agreeable and generous host. As for himself, he was very abstemious. He had been at one period of his life a decided dyspeptic, and was always obliged to be very careful of his diet.

* * *

After the return of the victorious army to its old quarters at Fredericksburg the remainder of May was consumed in recruiting and reorganizing. The infantry was formed into three corps of three divisions each . . . The organization of the cavalry remained unchanged, but that of the artillery demanded the special attention of the commander-in-chief . . . The plan . . . adopted was to group the artillery of the army into battalions of four batteries each. . . .

By the 1st of June the reconstruction and equipment of the army was completed, and the Army of Northern Virginia appeared the best disciplined, the most high-spirited, and enthusiastic army on the continent. It consisted of 52,000 infantry, 250 pieces of artillery, and 9000 cavalry, making an aggregate force of 65,000 men. The successful campaign which this army had recently passed through inspired it with almost invincible ardor. This splendid result had been accomplished by the almost unaided efforts of General Lee.

* * *

ABOVE: A stone marker at the spot where General Jackson fell.

LEFT: Enlistees departing near Falmouth, Virginia, after the Chancellorsville campaign.

Chapter VI

Gettysburg

By the first of June General Lee had completed his arrangements for the ensuing campaign. The army, though numerically less than it was when he commenced his operations against McClellan on the Chickahominy, had been by its recent victories imbued with a confidence that greatly increased its efficiency. Its spirit was now high, and it was anxious to grapple again its powerful foe, which still lingered on the Stafford Heights.

The object of the campaign being the defence of Richmond, General Lee could either continue on the defensive and oppose the Federal advance as he had recently done, or he might assume the offensive and by bold manoeuvring oblige the Federal army to recede from its present line of operations to protect its capital or oppose the invasion of Maryland or Pennsylvania.

The advance upon Richmond would thus be frustrated, and the attack upon that city delayed, at least for a time. The dispirited condition of the Federal army since its late defeat, and the high tone of that of the Confederates, induced the adoption of the latter plan.

This decision was reached by General Lee near the close of May and after the completion of the reorganization of the army which followed the battle of Chancellorsville. Before the movement began his plans of operation were fully matured, and with such precision that the exact locality at which a conflict with the enemy was expected to take place was indicated on his map. This locality was the town of Gettysburg, the scene of the subsequent great battle.

At the period mentioned he called the

BELOW: General Hooker's army marching past Manassas, Va. in June 1863. General Lee rejected suggestions that he engage the Army of the Potomac here.

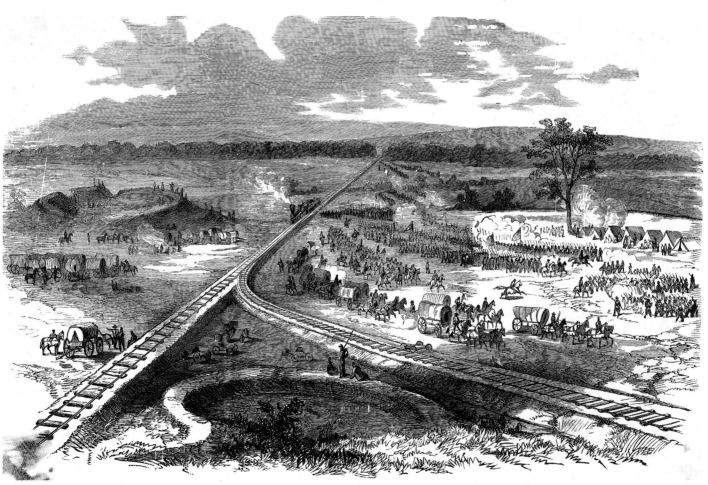

writer into his tent, headquarters being then near Fredericksburg. On entering I found that he had a map spread on the table before him, which he seemed to have been earnestly consulting. He advised me of his designed plan of operations, which we discussed together and commented upon the probable result. He traced on the map the proposed route of the army and its destination in Pennsylvania, while in his quietly effective manner he made clear to me his plans for the campaign. He first proposed, in furtherance of his design, to manoeuvre the army in such a way as to draw Hooker from the Rappahannock. At this point in the conversation I suggested that it might be advantageous to bring Hooker to an engagement somewhere in the vicinity of the old battlefield of Manassas. To this idea General Lee objected, and stated as his reason for opposing it that no results of decisive value to the Confederate States could come from a victory in that locality. The Federal army, if defeated, would fall back to the defences of Washington, as on previous occasions, where it could reorganize in safety and again take the field in full force.

In his view, the best course would be to invade Pennsylvania, penetrating this State in the direction of Chambersburg, York, or Gettysburg. He might be forced to give battle at one or the other of these places as circumstances might suggest, but, in his view, the vicinity of Gettysburg was much the best point, as it was less distant from his base on the Potomac, and was so situated that by holding the passes of the South Mountain he would be able to keep open his line of communication. York, being some twenty-five miles farther from the mountains, was a less desirable locality.

In this plan he had a decided object. There was in his mind no thought of reaching Philadelphia, as was subsequently feared in the North. Yet he was satisfied that the Federal army, if defeated in a pitched battle, would be seriously disorganized and forced to retreat across the Susquehanna – an event which would give him control of Maryland and Western Pennsylvania, and probably of West Virginia, while it would very likely cause the fall of Washington City and the flight of the Federal Government. Moreover, an important diversion would be

ABOVE: Union cavalrymen of the 3rd Pennsylvannia, commanded by Alfred Pleasonton, photographed at Gettysburg.

RIGHT: General Richard S. Ewell commanded the Second Corps of Confederate infantry. A. P. Hill had the First Corps and Longstreet the Third Corps. Jeb Stuart was commander of the cavalry.

made in favor of the Western department, where the affairs of the Confederacy were on the decline. These highly important results, which would in all probability follow a successful battle, fully warranted, in his opinion, the hazard of an invasion of the North.

The plan which he thus indicated was already fully matured in his own mind, and the whole line of movement was laid down on the map. He alluded to the several strategic points in Maryland, but did not think it would be advisable to make any stand in that State, for the same reason as before given. This interview took place about two weeks before the movement began. The proposed scheme of operations was submitted to President Davis in a personal interview, and fully approved by him.

*   *   *

BELOW: Shelling Confederate rifle pits on the Rappahannock on June 5, prior to a crossing by the Union VI Corps under John Sedgwick.

On the 2d of June, Ewell's corps, preceded by the cavalry, was sent forward to Culpeper Court-house. A day or two after, Longstreet, accompanied by the commander-in-chief, followed Ewell, while Hill remained at Fredericksburg to observe the movements of Hooker. By the 8th of June

the main body of the Confederate army was concentrated in the neighborhood of Culpeper and the Federal army was in motion for the upper Rappahannock. . . . On the 10th, Ewell was advanced toward the Shenandoah Valley, both for the purpose of expelling from that section a considerable Federal force, and to create an impression of

a flank movement with the view of interrupting Hooker's communications. . . . Hooker suddenly withdrew from the Rappahannock and retired to the vicinity of Manassas and Centreville, where he assumed a defensive attitude for the protection of Washington. Thus by a series of bold strategic movements General Lee removed the enemy from his path and accomplished the . . . extension of his line from Fredericksburg to Winchester in the face of an enemy of more than double his numerical strength.

* * *

On the 15th, Longstreet was put in motion for the Valley, and Hill was directed to follow a day later, . . . General Lee arrived with Longstreet's corps at Berryville on the 18th, . . . About the 21st he continued his advance in two columns: the one, composed of the corps of Ewell and Hill, was directed to Shepherdstown, and the other, consisting of Longstreet's corps and the supply-train, proceeded to Williamsport. Ewell crossed the Potomac on the 23d, followed by Hill on the 24th, while its passage was effected by Longstreet and the trains on the 25th at Williamsport.

As Lee's plan of operations unfolded itself, Hooker advanced to the Potomac and took possession of the fords in the neighborhood of Leesburg. When he learned that Lee had entered Maryland he immediately crossed the river and advanced to Frederick. A controversy then occurred between Halleck and himself, which resulted in his removal on the 27th and the placing of General Meade in command of the Army of the Potomac.

* * *

Immediately on completing the passage of the Potomac, Lee resumed his advance, directing Ewell to Carlisle, while he proceeded with Longstreet and Hill to Chambersburg. Ewell sent Early to York by way of Gettysburg, and then moved with the rest of his corps, accompanied by Jenkins's cavalry, to Carlisle. . . . Such was the disposition of the Confederate army during the latter part of June.

* * *

Lee first learned of the appointment of General Meade to the command of the Federal army on the 28th of June. . . . On reaching Chambersburg, General Lee . . . was

BELOW: Artillery going into action on the south bank of the Rappahannock on June 4.

ABOVE: War council of
General Meade and his
officers before the Battle of
Gettysburg.

OPPOSITE TOP: The death of
General John F. Reynolds,
Commander of the Federal I
Corps, on June 1.

OPPOSITE BOTTOM: Map of the
three-day Battle of
Gettysburg.

under the impression that the Federal army had not yet crossed the Potomac. It was not until the night of the 28th that he learned that the enemy had reached Frederick. . . .

The rapid advance of General Meade was unexpected, and exhibited a celerity that had not hitherto been displayed by the Federal army. A speedy concentration of the Confederate army was now necessary. Before dawn on the morning of the 29th orders were despatched requiring the immediate junction of the army, and on the 30th the Confederate forces were in motion toward Gettysburg. At the same time General Meade was pressing forward for that place.

This movement of the Confederate army began with the advance of A. P. Hill's corps, which bivouacked near Greenville on the night of the 29th, and reached Cashtown during the next day. Orders had been sent to Ewell to recall his advanced divisions and concentrate in the same locality. Longstreet's corps followed on the 30th, accompanied by headquarters, and encamped that night near the western base of South Mountain, in the neighborhood of the Stevens furnace. On July 1st he advanced to

Cashtown, a locality about six miles from Gettysburg.

While Lee and his staff were ascending South Mountain firing was heard from the direction of Gettysburg. This caused Lee some little uneasiness. The unfortunate absence of the cavalry prevented him from knowing the position and movements of the enemy, and it was impossible to estimate the true condition of affairs in his front. He was at first persuaded that the firing indicated a cavalry affair of minor importance, but by the time Cashtown was reached the sound had become heavy and continuous, and indicated a severe engagement.

General Lee now exhibited a degree of anxiety and impatience, and expressed regret at the absence of the cavalry. He said that he had been kept in the dark ever since crossing the Potomac, and intimated that Stuart's disappearance had materially hampered the movements and disorganized the plans of the campaign.

In a short time, however, his suspense was relieved by a message from A. P. Hill, who reported that he was engaged with two corps of the enemy, and requested reinforcements. Anderson's division, which

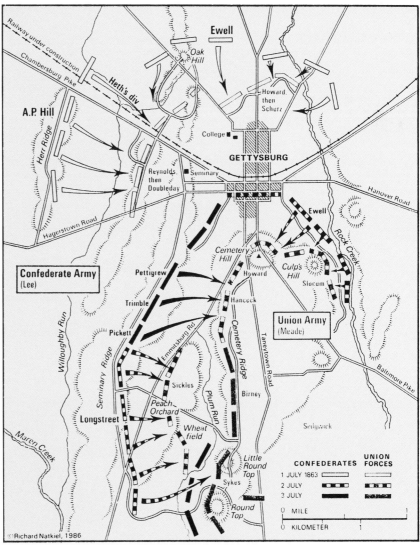

had just reached Cashtown, was at once pushed forward to his support, and General Lee with his staff quickly followed.

The situation in front at that time was as follows: During the forenoon of July 1st the two leading corps of the Federal army, commanded by General Reynolds, had arrived at Gettysburg; at the same time the heads of Hill's and Ewell's corps were rapidly approaching. About ten o'clock, General Heth of Hill's corps encountered a part of Buford's cavalry, which had been thrown forward on the Chambersburg road to a small stream called Willoughby Run, three miles from Gettysburg. Having driven back Buford, Heth engaged Wadsworth's division of the First corps, which was soon reinforced by other divisions of that corps, while Heth was supported by Pender's division of Hill's corps. The advance of the Eleventh corps (Howard's) and the arrival of Rodes's and Early's divisions of Ewell's corps, increased the proportions of the combat, which quickly became animated and continued with spirit until about four o'clock in the afternoon, when the Federal corps were totally defeated and driven from the field with very heavy loss. General Reynolds was killed, and his two corps were seriously reduced in numbers and greatly disorganized. The Confederate loss was much

RIGHT: General George Gordon Meade was appointed to replace General Hooker as Army of the Potomac commander on June 28, only a few days before the start of the Battle of Gettysburg.

smaller than that of the enemy; nevertheless, the fall of many gallant soldiers was to be regretted. Among the wounded was the gallant General Heth, whose command suffered severely.

Near the close of the action General Lee reached the field. Anderson's division came up soon afterward, and about the same time Longstreet arrived in advance of his corps, which was a few miles behind. As the troops were evidently very much fatigued, and somewhat disorganized by rapid marching and hard fighting, it seemed inadvisable to immediately pursue the advantage which had been gained, particularly as the retreating forces of the enemy were known to have been reinforced, and to have taken a defensive position about a mile south of the town.

This subject occupied Lee's attention upon perceiving the situation of affairs and

the victory gained by his advance forces, and he entered into a conversation with Longstreet, in the presence of the writer, concerning the relative positions of the two armies and the movements it was advisable to make. Longstreet gave it as his opinion that the best plan would be to turn Meade's left flank and force him back to the neighborhood of Pipeclay Creek. To this General Lee objected, and pronounced it impracticable under the circumstances.

At the conclusion of the conversation Colonel Long was directed to make a reconnoissance of the Federal position on Cemetery Ridge, to which strong line the retreating troops had retired. This he did, and found that the ridge was occupied in considerable force. On this fact being reported to General Lee, he decided to make no farther advance that evening, but to wait till morning before attempting to follow up his advantage. This decision the worn-out condition of his men and the strength of the position held by the enemy rendered advisable. He turned to Longstreet and Hill, who were present, and said, "Gentlemen, we will attack the enemy in the morning as early as practicable." In the conversation that succeeded he directed them to make the necessary preparations and be ready for prompt action the next day. Longstreet's corps was at that time near Cashtown, but bivouacked for the night on Willoughby's Creek, about four miles from the battlefield.

I will here add that Gettysburg affords a good example of the difficulties to be encountered and the uncertainty of being able to harmonize the various elements of armies when the field of operations is extensive. This battle was precipitated by the absence of information which could only be obtained by an active cavalry force. General Lee had previously considered the possibility of engaging the enemy in the vicinity of Gettysburg, but the time and position were to have been of his own selection. This could have been easily effected had not the cavalry been severed from its proper place with the army.

At a later hour in the evening than that of the events above mentioned the writer had a further conversation with General Lee, which is of sufficient interest to be here narrated. We were then together at the bivouac, under the trees of an apple orchard.

The general, as if he had been thinking over his plans and orders, turned to me with the remark, "Colonel Long, do you think we had better attack without the cavalry? If we do so, we will not, if successful, be able to reap the fruits of victory."

"In my opinion," I replied, "it would be best not to wait for Stuart. It is uncertain where he is or when he will arrive. At present only two or three corps of the enemy's army are up, and it seems best to attack them before they can be greatly strengthened by reinforcements. The cavalry had better be left to take care of itself."

General Lee evidently agreed with me in this opinion. Much as he had been annoyed and his movements hampered by Stuart's absence, the condition of affairs was such that but one judicious course was open. An attack in force on the enemy before he could concentrate his army was very promising of success, and it was with this purpose fully determined upon in the general's mind that the events of that day ended for the Confederate army.

At this stage of the campaign the Count of Paris alludes to the tactics and strategy of

BELOW: Gettysburg and the Baltimore Pike, from Cemetery Hill.

ABOVE: Mrs. Thompson's house, General Lee's headquarters on the Chambersburg Pike.

General Lee in a tone of criticism which calls for some rejoinder on our part. He remarks:

He has four alternatives to select from: He has the choice to retire into the gaps of the South Mountain, in order to compel Meade to come after him; or to wait steadily in his present positions for the attack of the Federals; or, again, to manoeuvre in order to dislodge them from those they occupy by menacing their communications by the right or left; or, finally, to storm these positions in front, in the hope of carrying them by main force. The best plan would undoubtedly have been the first, because, by preserving the strategic offensive, Lee would thus secure all the advantages of the tactical defensive.

Could the count have seen the actual field of operation and have known the circum-

stances that governed General Lee, he would probably have taken a different view of his actions.

It must be borne in mind that in entering Pennsylvania without his cavalry General Lee was unable to accumulate supplies. In fact, the subsistence of his army mainly depended on the provisions that could be collected in the vicinity of his line of march by detachments of infantry mounted on artillery- and wagon-horses. Therefore, if Lee had adopted the count's preferred plan of operation and occupied one of the passes of South Mountain, he would have placed his army in a trap that would have, in the absence of a miracle, resulted in its destruction; for Meade with his superior forces could have enclosed him without supplies or the means of obtaining them. Lee would thus have been reduced to the alternative of laying down his arms or of cutting his way

out with great sacrifice of life and the loss of his artillery and transportation.

The above objection is also applicable to the count's second plan, with the addition that General Lee's line was too much extended to admit of a successful defence against General Meade's superior force. In answer to the count's third plan, it is only necessary to say that the proximity of the two armies and the absence of cavalry on the part of the Confederates rendered manoeuvring impracticable. The fourth is the only one that admitted of the hope of success, and was the one adopted by General Lee.

That the battle may be more clearly described it is necessary to present some of the principal topographical features of the neighborhood of Gettysburg. The town of Gettysburg, nestling in a small valley, is surrounded by numerous low ridges making

various angles with each other. The most important of them is the one situated about a mile south-west, known as Cemetery Ridge. It is terminated by two conical mounds about four miles apart. The one to the south is designated the Round Top. The one to the north is called Culp's Hill.

Immediately after the defeat of the First and Eleventh corps Cemetery Ridge was selected as the Federal position. Nearer the town is a second ridge, nearly parallel to, and about a thousand yards west of, the Cemetery Ridge. This ridge during the battle formed the Confederate centre. From its southern extremity springs obliquely a spur extending almost on a line with the Round Top. This naturally formed the Confederate right. East of the town the valley is traversed by a small stream, beyond which rises abruptly a commanding ridge which was occupied by the Confederate left. The more

ABOVE: Gatehouse to Evergreen Cemetery built at the summit of Cemetery Hill. Union troops fired at attacking Southerners from behind gravestones here.

ABOVE: General J. E. B. Stuart's cavalry was prevented from joining Lee at Gettysburg until July 2.

Maryland and Pennsylvania before he could resume his proper place with the army. This occupied him seven or eight days, and it was the 2d of July before he rejoined the army at Gettysburg in a very reduced condition, for many of his men had been dismounted, and the horses of those who remained in the saddle were much jaded by long and rapid marches. Notwithstanding the bad plight of his cavalry, Stuart, with his usual promptitude, placed it on the flanks of the army, where its presence was much needed. On the 3d it engaged the enemy's cavalry in frequent skirmishes and several fierce encounters, in one of which General Hampton was severely wounded.

The divisions of Robertson and Jones, which had been ordered up from the passes of the Blue Ridge, did not reach the army in time to take part in the battles of the 1st and 2d, and were too late to be of any service in preliminary reconnoissances. In consequence of these facts, General Lee in the whole of this campaign was deprived of the use of that portion of his force which has been truly named "the eye of the army," since without it all movements are made in the dark and the army is forced to grope its way forward.

At an early hour on the morning of the 2d the writer (Colonel Long) was directed to examine and verify the position of the Confederate artillery. He accordingly examined the whole line from right to left, and gave the necessary instructions for its effective service. As the morning advanced surprise began to be felt at the delay in commencing the attack on the right, which had been ordered to take place at an early hour. The object was to dislodge the Federal force, that had retreated after its defeat to the position known as Cemetery Ridge, before it could be reinforced to any considerable extent. By so doing Lee hoped to be able to defeat the Federal army in detail before it could be concentrated. Ewell was directed to take a position opposite the eastern termination of Cemetery Ridge, while Hill occupied the ridge parallel to it; and Longstreet, whose corps had bivouacked four miles in the rear, was to move early the next morning and assail the Federal left, while Ewell was to favor his attack by an assault upon the Federal right. Hill was to hold himself in readiness to throw his strength where it would have the greatest effect.

After completing the duties assigned him, Colonel Long returned to join General Lee,

distant view is bounded by South Mountain and its projecting spurs.

As we have said so much in regard to the absence of the cavalry and the difficulties thence arising, it is proper at this point to explain its cause. Stuart's passage of the Potomac at a point eastward of that where the Federal crossing was made was intended, as has been said, as a feint, with the view of creating a diversion in favor of General Lee by arousing fears of danger to Washington, to the vicinity of which city the cavalry advanced. However, the movement proved a highly unfortunate one, and was followed by irretrievable disaster; for Stuart had no sooner entered Maryland than his return was barred by the intrusion of a large Federal force between him and the river, and he was thus obliged to make a wide circuit through

whom he met at Ewell's headquarters about 9 A.M. As it appeared, the general had been waiting there for some time, expecting at every moment to hear of the opening of the attack on the right, and by no means satisfied with the delay. After giving General Ewell instructions as to his part in the coming engagement, he proceeded to reconnoitre Cemetery Ridge in person. He at once saw the importance of an immediate commencement of the assault, as it was evident that the enemy was gradually strengthening his position by fresh arrivals of troops, and that the advantage in numbers and readiness which the Confederate army possessed was rapidly disappearing.

Lee's impatience increased after this reconnoissance, and he proceeded in search of Longstreet, remarking, in a tone of uneasiness, "What *can* detain Longstreet? He ought to be in position now." This was about 10 A.M.

After going some distance he received a message that Longstreet was advancing. This appeared to relieve his anxiety, and he proceeded to the point where he expected the arrival of the corps. Here he waited for some time, during which interval he observed that the enemy had occupied the Peach Orchard, which formed a portion of the ground that was to have been occupied by Longstreet. This was that advance movement of Sickles's command which has given rise to so much controversy among Federal historians.

General Lee, on perceiving this, again expressed his impatience in words and renewed his search for Longstreet. It was now about 1 o'clock P.M. After going some distance to the rear, he discovered Hood's division at a halt, while McLaws was yet at some distance on the Fairfield road, having taken a wrong direction. Longstreet was present, and with General Lee exerted himself to correct the error, but before the corps could be brought into its designated position it was four o'clock. The hope that had been entertained of taking the enemy at a disadvantage and defeating him in detail no longer existed. The whole of the Federal force, except Sedgwick's corps, was strongly posted on Cemetery Ridge. Sedgwick, whose corps had made a march of thirty-five miles in twenty hours, had reached the field, though his men were too much exhausted by the length and rapidity of their march to be of immediate service. Yet the opportunity which the early morning had presented was

lost. The entire Army of the Potomac was before us!

General Longstreet has published an explanation of the causes of this unfortunate, if not fatal, delay in the arrival of his troops, yet it cannot be said that the reason which he gives is entirely satisfactory. He says that on the 1st of July the march of his corps had been greatly delayed by the occupation of the road by a division of the Second corps and its wagon-trains. Yet his whole force, except Law's brigade, had reached a position within four miles of Gettysburg by midnight. On the next day, "Fearing that my force was too weak to venture to make an attack, I delayed until General Law's brigade joined its division. As soon after his arrival as we could make our preparations the movement began. Engineers sent out by the command-

ABOVE: On July 2, Lieutenant General James ("Old Pete") Longstreet's divisions were late in arriving at their designated positions but were nevertheless able to attack within the hour.

ing general and myself guided us by a road which would have completely disclosed the move. Some delay ensued in seeking a more concealed route. McLaws's division got into position opposite the enemy's left about 4 P.M. Hood's division was moved on farther to our right, and got into position, partially enveloping the enemy's left."

This explanation, as we have said, is not satisfactory. Longstreet, as he admits, had received instructions from Lee to move *with that portion of his command which was up*, to gain the Emmettsburg road. These orders he took the responsibility of postponing on account of the absence of one brigade of his command, so that, instead of being in readiness to attack in the early morning, it was four o'clock in the afternoon when his troops reached the field.

BELOW: In the afternoon of July 2, Major General John Bell Hood's division made the first assault, against a Union corps under Sickles, in a dash for Little Round Top.

He now found the position which had been laid out for him occupied by Sickles's corps of the Federal army, which had pushed forward considerably in advance of the line of Cemetery Ridge and taken position on the lower ridge along which ran the Emmettsburg road. Cemetery Ridge at this portion of its extent is ill defined, and the movement of Sickles to occupy the advanced position was not without tactical warrant. Yet it was faulty, from the fact that his line, to gain a defensive position for its left flank, had to be bent at a considerable angle at the advanced point known as the "Peach Orchard." General Humphreys's division occupied the road, while Birney's division held the salient point at the Peach Orchard, and was stretched back through low ground of woods and wheatfields toward Round Top, near which the left flank rested in a rocky ravine.

The weak point in this line was the salient at the Peach Orchard, which formed the key of Sickles's position; and on this, when the columns of Longstreet's corps moved to the attack at 4.30 P.M., the greatest vigor of the assault felt. The first assault, however, was made by Hood's division, which attacked the left wing of Sickles's corps, extending from the Peach Orchard to the vicinity of the two elevations known as Round Top and Little Round Top.

Through an interval which lay between Sickles's left and the foot of Round Top, Hood's extreme right thrust itself unperceived by the Federals, and made a dash for Little Round Top, which, through some strange oversight, was at this moment quite unoccupied by any portion of Meade's army. The elevation known by this name is a bold spur of the loftier height called Round Top. It is very rough and rugged, covered with massive boulders, and rendered difficult of ascent by its steepness and its outcropping granite ledges. Yet it was the keypoint of that whole section of the battlefield, and had Hood dreamed of its being unoccupied, pushed a powerful force in that direction, and seized the commanding summit, the victory would have been in his grasp, since the possession of this point would not only have placed Sickles's corps in a highly perilous position, but have enabled him to take the entire line in reverse.

It was at this critical moment that the Federals discovered their error and hastened to amend it. The prompt energy of a single officer, General Warren, chief engineer of

BELOW: Union Brigadier General Gouverneur K. Warren, Meade's chief engineer, commandeered a force to defend Little Round Top against Hood's Texans.

the army, rescued Meade's army from imminent peril. He had reached Little Round Top at the point of time in which Hood's men penetrated the undefended space between Sickles's left and Round Top, and just as the signal-officers who occupied the summit were folding up their flags preparatory to leaving the dangerous situation. Directing them to continue waving their flags, Warren hastened away in search of some available force to hold the hill, and, meeting a division of Sykes's corps which was marching to the support of Sickles's command, he detached from it Vincent's brigade, which he hurried to the threatened summit. A battery also, with great difficulty, was dragged and lifted to the top of the rugged hill.

It was a desperate rush from both sides for the possession of the important point, and the Federal brigade reached the crest just as the gallant Texans of Hood's division were swarming up the rocky slope with shouts of triumph. There ensued a desperate struggle for the contested summit. A severe volley from the Federals met Hood's men full in the face as they climbed the steep acclivity. The fight quickly became a hand-to-hand conflict, in which levelled bayonet and clubbed musket did their share in the work of death. For half an hour the contest continued. But the advantage of the Federals in their possession of the summit was not to be overcome, and, though the brave Texans stubbornly held the rocky glen at the foot of the

ABOVE: Atop Cemetery Ridge, Federal troops and artillery repulse a charge by Longstreet's exhausted troops.

hill, and worked their way up the ravine between the two elevations, they were eventually forced back by the Federals, though not without causing heavy loss to the latter. The error which had been made by the Federals was immediately retrieved by the reinforcement of Vincent's brigade, while Round Top was occupied at a later hour in the evening.

While this desperate struggle was in progress the assault on Sickles's corps was vigorously pressed by McLaws's division, particularly at the salient in the Peach Orchard, which was evidently the weak point of the line. The Federal resistance was stubborn, and reinforcements were hurried up to the imperilled point; yet the Confederate onslaught proved irresistible, pushing the line back to a wheatfield in the rear of the Peach Orchard, and eventually breaking it and hurling the enemy in disordered flight toward the high grounds in the rear.

This success rendered the Federal position untenable. The flanks of the broken line were exposed right and left, and, though reinforcements were in rapid succession hurried to the front, the whole line was gradually forced back toward Cemetery Ridge, leaving the hotly-contested field stewn with thousands of dead and wounded. Thus, after

a severe conflict for several hours, Longstreet had gained the position which he could have occupied earlier in the day without opposition. His advantage had not been gained without heavy loss, and, though the Confederates had gained the base of Cemetery Ridge, its crest was crowned with troops and artillery too strongly placed to be driven out by Longstreet's men in their exhausted condition.

A desperate effort to carry the ridge was made, but it proved unsuccessful, and the battle on that part of the line ended without a decisive result. It had been contested with great determination, and the loss on both sides had been heavy, but the Confederate success had consisted in driving the Federals out of an intrinsically weak position, while the strong defensive line of Cemetery Ridge remained intact in their hands. Whether the result would have been different had the original assault been made on this line is a question which it is impossible now to answer, and the advantage or disadvantage of Sickles's advance movement cannot be determined except from the standpoint of military strategy.

During Longstreet's assault on the right Hill's corps had made strong demonstrations against the Federal centre, but Ewell's demonstration on the left, which was ordered to be made at the same time, was delayed, and the corps only got fairly to work about sunset. The assault was maintained with great spirit by the divisions of Early and Edward Johnson until after dark. Early carried Cemetery Ridge, but was forced to relinquish it by superior numbers. The left of Ewell's corps penetrated the breastworks on the extreme right of the Federal line, and this position was held during the night. The ill-success of Early's movement was due to lack of support, the columns on his right failing to reach the contested point until after he had been forced to relinquish the position he had gained on the crest and retire to his original ground.

In the words of Colonel Taylor, "The whole affair was disjointed. There was an utter absence of accord in the movements of the several commands, and no decisive results attended the operations of the second day." This discordance was one of the unfortunate contingencies to which every battle is subject, and is in no sense chargeable to General Lee, whose plan had been skilfully laid, and had it been carried out in strict accordance with his instructions would probably have led to a very different result. On both sides the disregard by corps commanders of the express intentions of their superiors had changed the conditions of the battle. Sickles's advance beyond the position designed to be held by General Meade had exposed his corps to repulse and heavy loss, which possibly might have been avoided had he held the line of Cemetery Ridge, while Longstreet's assumption of the responsibility of delaying the assault ordered certainly had a most important influence on the result of the battle.

The dawn of the 3d of July found the two armies in the position in which the battle of the preceding day had ended. Though Cemetery Ridge remained intact in the hands of the Federals, yet the engagement had resulted at every point in an advantage to the Confederates. Longstreet had cleared his front of the enemy, and occupied the ground from which they had been driven. Ewell's left held the breastworks on Culp's Hill on the extreme right of the Federal line. Meade's army was known to have sustained heavy losses. There was, in consequence, good reason to believe that a renewed

BELOW: Field sketch made on July 2 of an officer assisting his men in repositioning a gun during the battle.

ABOVE: Confederates renewing their attack on Culp's Hill on the morning of the third day.

assault might prove successful. Ewell's position of advantage, if held, would enable him to take the Federal line in reverse, while an advance in force from Longstreet's position offered excellent promise of success. General Lee therefore determined to renew the assault.

Longstreet, in accordance with this decision, was reinforced, and ordered to assail the heights in his front on the morning of the 3d, while Ewell was directed to make a simultaneous assault on the enemy's right. Longstreet's dispositions, however, were not completed as early as those of Ewell, and the battle opened on the left before the columns on the right were ready to move. Johnson, whose men held the captured breastworks, had been considerably reinforced during the night, and was on the point of resuming the attack when the Federals opened on him at four o'clock with a heavy fire of artillery which had been placed in position under cover of the darkness. An infantry assault in force followed, and, though Ewell's men held their ground with their usual stubbornness, and maintained

their position for four hours, they were finally forced to yield the captured breastworks and retire before the superior force of the enemy.

This change in the condition of affairs rendered necessary a reconsideration of the military problem, and induced General Lee, after making a reconnoissance of the enemy's position, to change his plan of assault. Cemetery Ridge, from Round Top to Culp's Hill, was at every point strongly occupied by Federal infantry and artillery, and was evidently a very formidable position. There was, however, a weak point upon which an attack could be made with a reasonable prospect of success. This was where the ridge, sloping westward, formed the depression through which the Emmettsburg road passes. Perceiving that by forcing the Federal lines at that point and turning toward Cemetery Hill the right would be taken in flank and the remainder would be neutralized, as its fire would be as destructive to friend as foe, and considering that the losses of the Federal army in the two preceding days must weaken its cohesion and

Caisson and battery horses. Scene of Pickett's charge. 2nd corps near E Jones. Gettysburg July 4th 1863.

ABOVE: The wreckage of a Union battery following the massive bombardment preceding Pickett's Charge.

consequently diminish its power of resistance, General Lee determined to attack at that point, and the execution of it was assigned to Longstreet, while instructions were given to Hill and Ewell to support him, and a hundred and forty-five guns were massed to cover the advance of the attacking column.

The decision here indicated was reached at a conference held during the morning on the field in front of and within cannon-range of Round Top, there being present Generals Lee, Longstreet, A. P. Hill, and H. Heth, Colonel A. L. Long, and Major C. S. Venable. The plan of attack was discussed, and it was decided that General Pickett should lead the assaulting column, to be supported by the divisions of McLaws and Hood and such other force as A. P. Hill could spare from his command. The only objection offered was by General Longstreet, who remarked that the guns on Round Top might be brought to bear on his right. This objection was answered by Colonel Long, who said that the guns on Round Top could be suppressed by our batteries. This point being

settled, the attack was ordered, and General Longstreet was directed to carry it out.

Pickett's division was fresh, having taken no part in the previous day's fight, and to these veterans was given the post of honor in the coming affray, which promised to be a desperate and terrible one.

About twelve o'clock the preparations for the attack were completed and the signal for battle was given, which was immediately followed by the concentrated fire of all the Confederate artillery on Cemetery Hill, which was promptly responded to by the powerful Federal batteries. Then ensued one of the most tremendous artillery engagements ever witnessed on an open field: the hills shook and quivered beneath the thunder of two hundred and twenty-five guns as if they were about to be torn and rent by some powerful convulsion. In the words of General Hancock in reference to the performance of the opposing batteries, "Their artillery fire was the most terrific cannonade I ever witnessed, and the most prolonged – . . . one possibly hardly ever paralleled."

For more than an hour this fierce artillery

Opening engagement.

Retiring with prolonge.

Shelled out.

Position on the 3rd and 4th July.

Leaving the field, July 5th.

conflict continued, when the Federal guns began to slacken their fire under the heavy blows of the Confederate batteries, and ere long sank into silence – an example which was quickly followed by the Confederates.

A deathlike stillness then reigned over the field, and each army remained in breathless expectation of something yet to come still more dreadful. In a few moments the attacking column, consisting of Pickett's division, supported on the left by that of Heth commanded by Pettigrew, and on the right by Wilcox's brigade of Anderson's division, appeared from behind a ridge, and, sweeping over its crest, descended into the depression that separated the two armies. The enemy for a moment seemed lost in admiration of this gallant array as it advanced with the steadiness and precision of a review. Their batteries then opened upon it a spasmodic fire, as if recovering from a stunning blow. The force that moved to the attack numbered about 15,000 men. It had a terrible duty to perform. The distance which it was obliged to traverse was more than half a mile in width, and this an open plain in full front of the enemy, who thickly crowded the

crest of the ridge, and within easy range of their artillery.

But the tempest of fire which burst upon the devoted column quickly reduced its strength. The troops of Heth's division, decimated by the storm of deadly hail which tore through their ranks, faltered and fell back in disorder before the withering volleys of the Federal musketry. This compelled Pender's division, which had marched out to support the movement, to fall back, while Wilcox, on perceiving that the attack had failed, fell back, after severe loss, leaving Pickett's men to continue the charge alone. The other supports, Hood's and McLaws's divisions, which had been expected to advance in support of the charging column, did not move, and were too remote to offer any assistance. The consequence was that Pickett was left entirely unsupported.

Yet the gallant Virginians marched steadily forward, through the storm of shot and shell that burst upon their devoted ranks, with a gallantry that has never been surpassed. As they approached the ridge their lines were torn by incessant volleys of musketry as by a deadly hail. Yet with un-

ABOVE: Assault and repulse of George Pickett's Virginians on Cemetery Hill.

OPPOSITE TOP: Scenes of Federal troops in the field, from the opening engagement, at upper left, to withdrawal on July 5, at lower right.

OPPOSITE BOTTOM: The artillery engagement at noon on the third day of battle.

faltering courage the brave fellows broke into the double-quick, and with an irresistible charge burst into the Federal lines and drove everything before them toward the crest of Cemetery Hill, leaping the breastworks and planting their standards on the captured guns with shouts of victory.

The success which General Lee had hoped and expected was gained, but it was a dearly-bought and short-lived one. His plan had gone astray through the failure of the supporting columns. Now was the time that they should have come to the aid of their victorious comrades; but, alas! Heth's division, which had behaved with the greatest gallantry two days before, had not been able to face the terrible fire of the Federal lines, while the other supports were too remote to afford timely relief. The victory which seemed within the grasp of the Confederate army was lost as soon as won. On every side the enemy closed in on Pickett's brigades, concentrating on them the fire of every gun in that part of their lines. It was impossible to long withstand this terrific fusillade. The band of heroes broke and fell back, leaving the greater part of their number dead or wounded upon the field or captive in the hands of their foes.

In justice to Heth's division it must be remembered that on the 1st it was the first to

attack the enemy, and maintain an unequal contest until it was reinforced by General Pender with his gallant North Carolinians, and a little later by two divisions of Ewell's corps, and that it continued to oppose the enemy with great gallantry to the close of the action, and suffered heavily both in officers and men, which greatly impaired on the 3d its usual firmness. The brigades of Pender's division had been heavily engaged both on the 1st and 2d, and on the 3d the brigades of Lane and Scales behaved with distinguished gallantry under General Trimble. Wilcox's brigade had gallantly supported Longstreet's attack on the afternoon of the 2nd, and on the 3rd was prevented by difficulties of the ground from keeping pace with the attacking column; and when it was seen that Pickett's attack had failed, it fell back in good order after having sustained heavy loss. All must admit that the troops from the different States were equally distinguished for valor and patriotism.

The Confederates lost in this attack about 4000 men, the most of whom were in Pickett's division. No troops could have behaved better than those of the Army of Northern Virginia on witnessing Pickett's repulse. The officers of every grade on that part of the field exerted themselves with the utmost coolness in preserving order and in

endeavoring to re-form the broken ranks, and the men so promptly obeyed the call to rally that their thin ranks were soon restored to order and the whole line was again established. The army was not discouraged or dispirited, and its sole wish was for an opportunity to efface the mortification of its first serious repulse. The desire was general that Meade should assume the offensive and in his turn make an attack, and no doubt was felt of the ability to give him a yet hotter reception than that which Pickett had received. But Meade found his army so much shattered and discouraged by his recent losses that he deemed it inadvisable to attempt to follow up his success.

That this view is correct is proved by the following passage from Mr. William Swinton's *History of the Army of the Potomac*. Mr. Swinton says:

I have become convinced from the testimony of General Longstreet himself that attack would have resulted disastrously. "I had," said that officer to the writer, "Hood and McLaws, who had not been engaged; I had a heavy force of artillery; I should have liked nothing better than to have been attacked, and have no doubt that I should have given those who tried as bad a reception as Pickett received."

OPPOSITE TOP: General Pickett receiving his orders to charge from General Longstreet.

OPPOSITE BOTTOM: At a point in the Union defenses known as the "Angle," General Lewis Armistead, his hat on his sword, destroys a Union battery before being cut down.

BELOW: Amputation at a Federal surgery at Gettysburg. In the fighting, the North suffered some 23,000 casualties and the South about 28,000, taking some 4000 casualties alone during Pickett's attack.

Mr. Swinton further informs us that besides the heavy loss it had sustained by Pickett's attack, the Army of the Potomac was thrown into much confusion by the intermingling of the troops of different divisions and corps. Among the wounded were Major-generals Hancock and Gibbon, two of its most prominent officers. The same writer also informs us that the aggregate loss of the Army of the Potomac during the three days' battle was 23,000 men. Among the officers killed was Major-general J. F. Reynolds, whose gentlemanly bearing and soldierly qualities were unsurpassed in any other officer of either army. In view of this heavy loss, while admitting that General Lee was defeated, it must be acknowledged that Generel Meade was so much crippled that he could not reap any advantage of victory.

The attack of Pickett's division on the 3d has been more criticised, and is still less understood, than any other act of the Gettysburg drama. General Longstreet did not enter into the spirit of it, and consequently did not support it with his wonted vigor. It has been characterized as rash and object-less, on the order of the "charge of the Light Brigade." Nevertheless, it was not ordered without mature consideration and on grounds that presented fair prospects of success. By extending his left wing west of the Emmettsburg road, Meade weakened his position by presenting a weak centre, which being penetrated, his wings would be isolated and paralyzed, so far as regarded supporting each other. A glance at a correct sketch of the Federal position on the 3d will sufficiently corroborate this remark, and had Pickett's division been promptly supported when it burst through Meade's centre, a more positive proof would have been given, for his right wing would have been overwhelmed before the left could have disengaged itself from woods and mountains and come to its relief.

Pickett's charge has been made the subject of so much discussion, and General Lee's intentions in ordering it have been so misunderstood, that it is deemed proper to here offer, in corroboration of what has been said above, the testimony of one who was thoroughly conversant with all the facts.

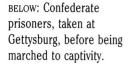

BELOW: Confederate prisoners, taken at Gettysburg, before being marched to captivity.

Colonel Walter H. Taylor, adjutant-general on the staff of General Lee, in *Southern Historical Society Papers*, vol. iv. p. 83, states as follows:

Later, General Lee rode over to General Ewell's front and conferred as to future movements. He wanted to follow up the success gained – thought that with Johnson's division, then up, that General Ewell could go forward at dawn next day. Ewell, Early, and Rodes thought it best to await Longstreet's arrival and make the main attack on the enemy's left. This was determined on. Longstreet was then about four miles off, with two of his divisions. He was expected early on the morning of the 2d. Orders were sent him to move up to gain the Emmettsburg road. He did not reach the field early, and his dispositions were not completed for attack until four o'clock in the afternoon. In his report General Longstreet says he received orders to move with the portion of his command that was then up, to gain the Emmettsburg road on the enemy's left, but, fearing that he was too weak to attack, he

delayed until one of his brigades (Law's) joined its division, and that he began the movement as soon after its arrival as his preparations would admit. It seemed impossible to get the co-operation of the commanders along the line. When Longstreet did attack, he did it in handsome style – drove the enemy and captured prisoners, artillery, and other trophies. So far, we had succeeded in every encounter with the enemy. It was thought that a continuance of the attack as made by Longstreet offered promise of success. He was ordered to renew the fight early on the 3d; Ewell, who was to co-operate, ordered Johnson to attack at an early hour, anticipating that Longstreet would do the same. Longstreet delayed. He found that a force of the enemy occupying high ground on their left would take his troops in reverse as they advanced. Longstreet was then visited by General Lee, and they conferred as to the mode of attack. It was determined to adhere to the plan proposed, and to strengthen him for the movement he was to be reinforced by Heth's division and two brigades of Pender's of Hill's

BELOW: Union soldiers killed in the first days' fighting lie near the Chambersburg Pike.

ABOVE: A young Confederate sniper lies dead in the Devil's Den, a sharpshooters nest at the foot of The Round Top.

corps. With his three divisions which were to attack Longstreet made his dispositions, and General Lee went to the centre to observe movements. The attack was not made as designed: Pickett's division, Heth's division, and two brigades of Pender's division advanced. Hood and McLaws were not moved forward. There were nine divisions in the army; seven were quiet, while two assailed the fortified line of the enemy. A. P. Hill had orders to be prepared to assist Longstreet further if necessary. Anderson, who commanded one of Hill's divisions and was in readiness to respond to Longstreet's call, made his dispositions to advance, but General Longstreet told him it was of no use – the attack had failed. Had Hood and McLaws followed or supported Pickett, and Pettigrew and Anderson been advanced, the design of the commanding general would have been carried out: the world would not

be so at a loss to understand what was designed by throwing forward, unsupported, against the enemy's stronghold so small a portion of our army. Had General Lee known what was to happen, doubtless he would have manoeuvred to force General Meade away from his strong position by threatening his communications with the East, as suggested by –; but he felt strong enough to carry the enemy's lines, and I believe success would have crowned his plan had it been faithfully carried out.

*   *   *

But one course remained open for General Lee. Retreat was necessary. . . . He had still an army of 50,000 men, unbroken in spirit and quite ready to sustain any attack which might be made upon them. But it was quickly evident that Meade had no intention of making an aggressive movement, and a renewed assault on the part of the Confederates would have been madness. . . .

Under these circumstances General Lee determined upon a retreat, but not such an immediate or hasty one as would present the appearance of flight. That he had deeply felt the failure of his effort is unquestionable, yet he preserved much of his ordinary calmness of demeanor, and not one word came from his lips to show that he laid blame on any subordinate . . . .

* * *

During the interval between the repulse of Pickett's charge and the night of July 4th . . . General Lee . . . caused the dead to be buried and the severely wounded to be carefully provided for. . . . When it became dark the withdrawal of the army began. First the trains, under protection of Hill's corps, moved out on the Fairfield road; Longstreet followed Hill; then came Ewell, bringing up the rear. The movement was so much impeded by soft roads, darkness, and rains that the rear-guard could not be withdrawn until daylight on the morning of the 5th. General Meade did not attempt to harass the retreating columns of Lee until the rear-guard had reached the neighborhood of Fairfield; then a pursuing column appeared on the neighboring heights, which Early promptly prepared to meet by throwing the rear-guard across its path. After exchanging a few shots the enemy retired, and the retreat was continued . . . .

* * *

BELOW: To cover Lee's retreat from Pennsylvannia, railroad tracks were destroyed.

RIGHT: General Meade's August encampment at Culpeper Court-house, Virginia.

The army bivouacked on the night of the 5th in South Mountain Pass, and on the morning of the 6th entered the rich and beautiful Cumberland Valley. . . . Reaching Williamsport on the 7th, and finding his pontoon bridge destroyed and the Potomac swollen far above the fording-point, General Lee occupied a strong position, covering Williamsport and Falling Waters, the point where he had left his bridge on advancing into Pennsylvania. As day after day passed without the appearance of the enemy, General Lee was able to complete his defences, so that when Meade arrived in force on the 12th the Army of Northern Virginia was eager to encounter its old antagonist, though double its numerical strength.

* * *

Notwithstanding the Army of the Potomac after its departure from Gettysburg was reinforced to its former numerical strength, General Meade did not attack, but employed the 12th and 13th in fortifying his position. On the other hand, General Lee, now that his bridge was finished and that the river had fallen so as to be fordable for cavalry and empty and lightly-loaded wagons, being unwilling to engage in a battle that could not promise important results, withdrew from his position on the night of the 13th, and retired across the Potomac. The movement was completed during the forenoon of the 14th without interruption, and the broad Potomac rolled between the hostile armies. . . . General Lee continued to retire slowly toward Winchester, and shortly after Meade moved down the river to the neighborhood of Harper's Ferry, and late in July entered Virginia east of the Blue Ridge, whereupon Lee withdrew from the Valley and took a position behind the Rapidan about the 1st of August, while General Meade occupied the neighborhood of Culpeper Court-house.

The losses of the army in killed, wounded, and prisoners were heavy, reaching nearly 16,000 men . . . Having placed the army in position on the Rapidan, and fearing the failure of his campaign in Pennsylvania might have caused the Confederate authorities to lose confidence in him, and feeling unwilling by retaining command of the army to embarrass them in their future plan of operations, General Lee sent his resignation to the President; which was, however, returned by Mr. Davis with every assurance of confidence.

* * *

Chapter VII

Wilderness, Spottsylvania, and Cold Harbor

For several weeks both armies remained inactive in the positions they had assumed – Lee on the Rapidan, and Meade in the vicinity of Culpeper Court-house. During that time so many convalescents and other absentees were restored to the ranks that the Army of Northern Virginia, with a small accession from other sources, was raised to a strength of nearly 60,000 men. . . . Within the same period two corps had been detached from the Federal army, . . . This reduction brought the opposing forces more nearly to a numerical equality than had previously been the case, and the change of conditions in his favor induced Lee to make an effort to force Meade to an engagement while his army was reduced in numbers.

* * *

In pursuance of his plan of operations, on the 9th of October Lee crossed the Rapidan. . . . Being much retarded by difficult roads, he did not reach his objective point near Culpeper Court-house until the afternoon of the 11th, too late to assail the Federal position that day. Meanwhile, Meade had become aware of the movement of the Confederate army. . . . On the approach of Lee his alert opponent had hastily retired, yet with such

skill that nothing of value was left behind. Lee's purpose of bringing the enemy to battle south of the Rappahannock had been foiled by this rapid retreat. ... There is reason to believe that Meade was as willing to accept battle as Lee was to offer it, but neither general had any desire to fight at a disadvantage, and a brisk series of manoeuvres for the advantage of position began.

*   *   *

On the morning of the 13th the Federal aramy was again concentrated on the north of the Rappahannock.

*   *   *

Meade had made the best use of the several unavoidable delays of the Confederate army, and though Hill, who was seeking to intercept the Federal retreat at Bristoe Station, made all haste in his march, he arrived there only in time to meet the rearguard of Meade's army. He made a prompt attack on the Federal column, which was hastening to pass Broad Run, which the remainder of the army had already crossed. The assault proved unfortunate. ... General

Cooke, who led the charging brigade, was severely wounded, and his command repulsed ... By the next morning the Federal army had crossed Bull Run, behind which they were erecting fortifications. Meade was safe from any further pursuit, with the intrenchments around Washington and Alexandria to fall back upon in the event of a repulse or to retire to if he wished to avoid a battle. Lee felt it expedient to withdraw, and after destroying the railroad from Cub Run to the Rappahannock, he retired on the 18th to the line of that river, leaving the cavalry in the enemy's front.

*   *   *

Lee remained on the Rappahannock until the railroad track was broken up and the rails removed for a distance extending from Catlett's Station to Culpeper Court-house. Meanwhile, the Federal army had again advanced, rapidly repairing the railroad as they moved forward, and on November 7th reached the Rappahannock. Lee's army was now encamped at Culpeper, with advanced forces near the river. ... Meade threw his whole army across the river and advanced on Culpeper, Lee retiring to his former posi-

BELOW: Northern soldiers and civilians on November 19 wait for a train to carry them to the dedication of the military cemetery at Gettysburg.

tion on the Rapidan. . . . The summer campaign having been one of unusual activity, and the late operations having entailed severe hardships, it was thought advisable to go into winter quarters, . . .

Yet Meade was not of this opinion. . . . Having failed to satisfy the expectations of the Washington authorities, Meade determined to strike a blow that might accomplish some desirable result. Therefore, about the last of November he advanced his entire force to Germanna Ford, hoping to cross the Rapidan at that point and surprise Lee in his extended winter quarters. . . . Meade began his march upon the Rapidan on November 26th. . . . Yet his advance had but fairly begun when the watchful Stuart discovered the movement, and hastened to report it to the Southern commander, who at once instituted measures for the rapid concentration of his army. . . .

Ewell's corps, which was at hand, was concentrated quickly, while Hill, who had from fifteen to twenty miles to march, was but a few hours later in taking his position. . . . Meanwhile, Meade's army was advancing in the lightest marching order. . . . Yet there were unforeseen causes of delay . . . so that by the time the river was crossed twenty-four hours had elapsed.

LEFT: Map of the Wilderness battlefield, an area familiar to Lee but unknown ground to General Grant.

This delay gave Lee all the time he needed. . . . In a remarkably short space of time an extended line of works was erected, composed of double walls of logs filled in with earth and with a strong abatis in front. The position had . . . become formidable.

* * *

It was a bitter disappointment to General Meade to find that his well-laid plans had been utterly foiled by the skill and alertness of his antagonist. The next two days were spent in reconnoitering movements, in hope of finding a favorable point of attack. On the 29th, Warren reported favorable conditions for assault on the Confederate right, while Sedgwick discovered what seemed a weak point on its left. Orders for an assault at both points on the next morning were accordingly given, and at the appointed time the artillery of the right and centre opened briskly on the Confederate lines.

But not a sound came from Warren on the left. A new conclusion had been reached in that quarter – a verdict of the men themselves. . . . As the hour for the assault arrived it was found that each man had pinned to his blue blouse a scrap of paper with his name written thereon, that he might be recognized by his friends in case of death. This signifi-

cant indication of the verdict of men whom long experience had made as expert military critics as their officers, was not to be disregarded. Warren, and after him Meade, made a new reconnoissance of the works before them, and the designed assault was pronounced hopeless. . . .

* * *

Finding that the enemy was not inclined to attack, Lee decided to give them a surprise, and to assail their lines on the morning of December 2nd. . . . But with the dawning of the next day it was discovered that . . . Meade's army was in full retreat toward the Rapidan. Pursuit was immediately made. But it was in vain. The light marching equipment of General Meade enabled him to far outstrip his pursuers. . . . The season was now so far advanced that neither general contemplated the prosecution of further operations during the winter; therefore preparations were commenced for going into winter quarters.

* * *

The hostile armies having remained opposed to each other for more than six months were aware that the ensuing campaign would be one of the most formidable

OPPOSITE TOP: Abraham Lincoln delivering his "little speech," the Gettysburg Address, before a crowd of 15,000.

OPPOSITE BOTTOM: Army winter quarters in Virginia.

ABOVE: Union General Benjamin Butler was supposed to support Grant's campaign against Lee by mounting a diversionary attack on Richmond from the Virginia peninsula. Like many other Butler operations, this one was mismanaged and failed to produce any useful result.

character. Therefore, each side made full use of its resources in preparation for the coming struggle. . . . In March, 1864, General Ulysses S. Grant was appointed lieutenant-general and assigned to the command of all the Federal armies. These were formed into two grand divisions. That of the West was assigned to the command of General Sherman, while that of the East was commanded by General Grant in person. Having established his headquarters with the Army of the Potomac, he applied himself to the study of the military situation in Virginia and . . . caused the Army of the Potomac to be raised to the imposing strength of 140,000 men, . . . General Lee . . . could only raise an effective force of 64,000 men. . . . In addition to the difference in numbers there was as marked

a difference in condition. The Army of the Potomac was well clothed and amply supplied. The Army of Northern Virginia was in ragged clothing and but half fed. . . . But, as on previous occasions of the kind, the soldiers were ready to fight. . . .

* * *

The new Federal general . . . determined on [a] southward movement through Virginia with his main army, while sending General Butler with 30,000 men to operate against Richmond from the James, and Sigel with a considerable force to advance through West Virginia and up the Shenandoah Valley.

Yet as the position of General Lee behind the Rappahannock was too strong to warrant a direct attack, . . . Grant [decided to cross] the Rapidan below Lee's right, and to endeavor to turn that flank of the Confederate army. This line, besides being shorter, possessed the advantage of preserving intact the communication with Washington, while it threatened to sever Lee's connection with Richmond.

The line being decided on and the necessary preparations being completed, General Meade on the 4th of May, under the eye of General Grant, put the Army of the Potomac in motion. The corps of Sedgwick and Warren moved forward on the road to Germanna Ford, while Hancock's corps proceeded to Ely's Ford, each column being preceded by a large force of cavalry. The passage of the river was effected without opposition.

This easy passage of the Rapidan does not seem to have been anticipated by General Grant. In his report he says: "This I regarded as a great success, and it removed from my mind the most serious apprehension I had entertained, that of crossing the river in the face of an active, large, well-appointed, and ably-commanded army." Lee had made no movement to dispute the passage of the stream. He could, had he chosen, have rendered its passage extremely difficult. But perceiving that Grant was making the mistake that had proved so disastrous to Hooker, by plunging with his army into that dense and sombre thicket well named "The Wilderness," he took care to do nothing to obstruct so desirable a result.

On reaching the southern side of the stream, Grant established himself at the intersection of the Germanna and old plank roads and at Chancellorsville. The position embraced the upper part of what is known as the Wilderness of Spottisylvania.

Lee simultaneously ordered the concentration of his forces on Mine Run, a position about four miles north-west of that occupied by Grant. The corps of Ewell and Hill and the artillery of Long and Walker gained their positions on Mine Run during the evening and night of the 4th; Longstreet's corps, which since its arrival from Tennessee had been posted at Gordonsville, distant twenty miles from the point of concentration, was necessarily delayed in reaching the scene of the coming struggle.

There seemed no good reason to believe that General Lee would risk the hazard of a battle in open field, and expose his small force to the danger of being overwhelmed by Grant's enormous army. That he would offer battle somewhere on the road to Richmond was unquestionable, but Grant naturally expected his adversary to select some point strong alike by nature and art, and which must be forced by sheer strength ere the march to Richmond could be resumed. He did not dream that Lee would himself make the attack and force a battle with no other intrenchments than the unyielding ranks of his veteran troops.

Yet Lee had already tried the woods of the Wilderness as a battlefield, and knew its advantages. Its intricacies, which were familliar to him and his generals, were unknown ground to Grant. In them he had already vanquished a large army with half its force. The natural hope of success in baffling his new opponent which this gave him he did not fail to avail himself of, and Grant found himself on his southward march unexpectedly arrested by the presence of the Confederate army in the wilds in which, just a year before, Hooker's confident army had been hurled back in defeat.

The writer spent the night of the 4th at Lee's headquarters, and breakfasted with him the next morning. The general displayed the cheerfulness which he usually exhibited at meals, and indulged in a few pleasant jests at the expense of his staff officers, as was his custom on such occasions. In the course of the conversation that attended the meal he expressed himself surprised that his new adversary had placed himself in the same predicament as "Fighting Joe" had done the previous spring. He hoped the result would be even more disastrous to Grant than that which Hooker had experienced. He was, indeed, in the best of spirits, and expressed much confidence in

the result – a confidence which was well founded, for there was much reason to believe that his antagonist would be at his mercy while entangled in these pathless and entangled thickets, in whose intricacies disparity of numbers lost much of its importance.

On the morning of the 5th, Lee's army advanced in two columns, Ewell taking the Orange Court-house and Fredericksburg turnpike, while Hill moved on the plank road. After advancing about three miles, Ewell encountered the enemy's outposts. Jones's brigade and a battery of artillery were then placed in position to cover the further deployment of Ewell's corps. Rodes's division formed in line to the right and at right angles to the road. The divisions of Early and Edward Johnson executed a similar deployment to the left.

Before this movement was finished Jones's brigade was ordered to change its position, and while in the execution of this was suddenly attacked by a heavy Federal force which had advanced unobserved under cover of a dense thicket. Before it could be extricated General Jones, its gallant leader, was killed, with the loss of several hundred of his men, either killed, wounded, or taken prisoner. This was the

BELOW: A view of the edge of the tangled area known as the Wilderness, in May 1864.

prelude to a succession of battles.

About four o'clock in the afternoon a collision occurred between the Federal right and the Confederate left. The hostile forces were concealed from view by a wilderness of tangled brushwood until they were within musket-range of each other. Then the Confederates, being in position, were prepared to deliver a staggering volley the moment their antagonists appeared, which was followed up so persistently that the Federals were driven back with heavy loss for nearly a mile. This affair closed the operations on the left.

On the right Hill met the enemy on the plank road and engaged in a heavy conflict. Hancock, who was opposed to him, made desperate efforts to drive him from his position, but in vain. "The assaults," as General Lee wrote, "were heavy and desperate, but every one was repulsed." Night fell, leaving both parties in the postiion which they held at the beginning of the fight. Neither had advanced or retired, but Hill had held his post and established his connection with Ewell.

The two armies had now assumed a most singular attitude. They had enveloped themselves in a jungle of tangled brushwood so dense that they were invisible to each other at half musket-range, and along the lines of a battle in many places objects were not discernible half the length of a battalion. A Northern writer aptly described this region as a "terra incognita." It formerly had been an extensive mining district, from which the timber had been cut to supply fuel for feeding the smelting-furnaces, and since then the young growth had sprung up ten times thicker than the primeval forest. The roads traversing it and the small brooks meandering through it, with a few diminutive clearings, were the only openings in this dismal wilderness.

As soon as General Grant had crossed the Rapidan and enveloped himself in the Wilderness of Spottsylvania, General Lee determined, as above said, to bring his adversary to an engagement in a position whose difficulties neutralized the vastly superior force against him. "Neither General Grant nor General Meade believed that aught but a small force was in front of Warren to mask the Confederate retreat, as it was not deemed possible that Lee, after his defensive line had been turned, could have acted with such boldness as to launch forward his army in an offensive sally. It was therefore at once resolved to brush away or capture this force, but as this determination was formed under a very erroneous apprehension of the actual situation, the means employed were inadequate to the task" (Swinton).

In corroboration of this statement may be quoted a remark ascribed to General Meade in conversaiion with Warren, Sedgwick, and others on the morning of the 5th: "They have left a division to fool us here, while they concentrate and prepare a position toward the North Anna; and what I want is to prevent those fellows from getting back to Mine Run."

Before nightfall of that day it was discovered that "those fellows" had other objects in view, and were not to be brushed away with a wave of the hand. Grant had become convinced that Lee was advancing upon him in force, and hastened to put his whole army in battle array. His line, crossing the plank road and old turnpike nearly at right angles, extended from Todd's Tavern on Brock road to within a short distance of Germanna Ford, presenting a front of about five miles.

General Lee had accompanied the advance of Hill on the plank road, and wit-

BELOW: Elements of the Army of the Potomac moving across the Rapidan and into the Wilderness.

nessed the noble firmness with which the divisions of Heth and Wilcox maintained the conflict against greatly superior odds until relieved by the coming of night. Perceiving that these troops had sustained considerable loss and were greatly fatigued by the exertions of the day, he wished to relieve them by Longstreet's corps, which had bivouacked during the evening about five miles from the field of battle. He therefore sent a message to General Longstreet to hurry him forward.

Notwithstanding the severe conflicts during the day, the troops of both Ewell and Hill maintained their unshaken courage, and lay upon their arms during the night in anticipation of a renewal of the attack.

Early on the following morning Hill's division was assailed with increased vigor, so heavy a pressure being brought to bear upon Heth and Wilcox that they were driven back, and, owing to the difficulties of the country, were thrown into confusion. The failure of Longstreet to appear came near causing a serious disaster to the army. But as this critical moment he arrived and attacked with such vigor that the enemy was driven back and the position regained.

Colonel C. S. Venable of General Lee's staff, in his address before the Southern Historical Society, thus describes this event:

The assertion, made by several writers, that Hill's troops were driven back a mile and a half is a most serious mistake. The right of his line was thrown back several hundred yards, but a portion of his troops still maintained their position. The danger, however, was great, and General Lee sent his trusted adjutant, Colonel W. H. Taylor, back to Parker's Store to get the trains ready for a movement to the rear. He sent an aide also to hasten the march of Longstreet's divisions. These came the last mile and a half at a double-quick, in parallel columns, along the plank road.

General Longstreet rode forward with that imperturbable coolness which always characterized him in times of perilous action, and began to put them in position on the right and left of the road. His men came to the front of the disordered battle with a steadiness unexampled even among veterans, and with an *élan* that presaged restoration of our position and certain victory. When they arrived the bullets of the enemy on our right flank had begun to sweep the field in the rear of the artillery-pits on the left

of the road, where General Lee was giving directions and assisting General Hill in rallying and re-forming his troops.

It was here that the incident of Lee's charge with Gregg's Texas brigade occurred. The Texans cheered lustily as their line of battle, coming up in splendid style, passed by Wilcox's disordered columns and swept across our artillery-pit and its adjacent breastwork. Much moved by the greeting of these brave men and their magnificent behavior, General Lee spurred his horse through an opening in the

ABOVE: A line of Confederates awaiting a Union advance in the Wilderness.

BELOW: Cadmus Marcellus Wilcox, whose greatly outnumbered men withstood repeated assaults by Federal troops until relieved by the arrival of Longstreet on the morning of May 6.

ABOVE: Troops of the 14th New York Infantry camped between a double line of breastworks on the night of May 6.

trenches and followed close on their line as it moved rapidly forward. The men did not perceive that he was going with them until they had advanced some distance in the charge. When they did recognize him, there came from the entire line as it rushed on the cry, "Go back, General Lee! go back!" Some historians like to put this in less homely words, but the brave Texans did not pick their phrases: "We won't go on unless you go back. . . ."

Just then I turned his attention to General Longstreet, whom he had been seeking, and who sat on his horse on a knoll to the right of the Texans directing the attack of his divisions. He yielded with evident reluctance to the entreaties of his men, and rode up to Longstreet's position. With the first opportunity I informed General Longstreet of what had just happened, and he with affectionate bluntness urged General Lee to go farther back. I need not say the Texans went forward in their charge and did well their duty. They were eight hundred strong, and lost half their number killed and wounded on that bloody day. The battle was soon restored and the enemy driven to his position of the night before.

Wilcox's and Heth's divisions, to whom Longstreet's arrival and General Lee's presence had done much to restore confi-

dence, were placed in line a short distance to the left of the plank road. Shortly afterward Anderson's division arrived from Orange Court-house. Longstreet now advanced from his own and Anderson's divisions three brigades to operate on the right flank of the enemy, while himself advancing on their front.

Attacked with great vigor by these fresh troops and his right flank rolled up at the same time that a heavy onslaught fell upon his front, Hancock's force was completely defeated, and sent reeling back toward the Brock road, the important highway to the seizure of which Lee's efforts were directed. That this purpose would be achieved seemed highly probable when an unfortunate accident put a stop to the Confederate advance. General Longstreet, who afterward declared that he "thought that he had another Bull Run on them," had ridden forward with his staff in front of his advancing line, when he was fired upon by a portion of his own flanking column, who mistook the party for Federal cavalry. He was struck by a musket-ball, and fell from his horse severely wounded.

This accident – which, as will be seen, bears a striking resemblance to that in which Lee's other great lieutenant, Jackson, was disabled in a previous battle in that same region – threw the lines into disorder and put a stop to the advance. General Lee, as soon as he learned of the accident, hastened to the spot to take command of the corps. But a considerable time elapsed before the divisions were ready for a renewal of the assault, and in the mean time the enemy had recovered from his confusion and had been strongly reinforced.

The battle was renewed about four o'clock in the afternoon, the columns of Longstreet and Hill, now commanded by Lee in person, making a most vigorous assault upon Hancock's men, who now lay intrenched behind a strongly-built breastwork of logs. The battle raged with great fury. The incessant volleys set fire to the woods, as at Chancellorsville, and flames and smoke soon filled the valley in which the contest was raging. The flames ere long caught to the breastworks of the enemy, which were soon a mass of seething fire. The battle went on through smoke and flame, and a portion of the breastworks were carried, though they were not long held. The few who had entered them were quickly driven out by a forward rush of a Federal brigade. With this charge ended the main action of the day.

In this engagement the attack of General Meade was conducted with such vigor by Hancock, Warren, and Burnside that under ordinary circumstances, with his great superiority of force, it would have been successful; but here the difficulties of the country prevented his making systematic combinations, and failure was the consequence.

While the battle was in progress on our right a spirited combat ensued between a part of Ewell's and Sedgwick's corps which terminated without important results. General Grant, being satisfied that any further attempt to dislodge Lee would be fruitless, determined to draw him out by a change of position. Therefore on the 7th he made his preparations to withdraw by night toward Spottsylvania Court-house.

* * *

The casualties of both armies during the 5th and 6th were heavy. The Confederates, besides the loss of 7000 men killed and wounded, had to lament the severe wound of General Longstreet, which disabled him during the remainder of the campaign. . . . The Federal loss was much greater.

* * *

Grant . . . designed by a rapid flank movement to seize the important position of Spottsylvania Court-house, fifteen miles south-east of the Wilderness battlefield. But [having] been informed by Stuart on the afternoon of the 7th that the wagon-trains of the Federal army were moving southward, Lee at once divined Grant's intention, and . . . placed his army, which was supposed to be fifteen miles in the rear, squarely across Grant's line of advance to Richmond. . . .

* * *

On the morning of the 10th, General Grant formed a powerful combination of the corps of Warren, Burnside, and Hancock with the design of attacking Lee's left centre near the point of junction of the corps of Longstreet and Ewell. . . . At five o'clock the main assault was made. Hancock's and Warren's men advanced with great intrepidity against the strong Confederate works, but were repulsed with terrible slaughter. . . . In the afternoon, . . . the Sixth corps made a heavy attack on Ewell's left. . . .

* * *

During the hottest portion of this engagement, when the Federals were pouring through the broken Confederate lines . . . Genereal Lee rode forward and took his position at the head of General Gordon's column, then preparing to charge. . . .

"No! no! General Lee to the rear! General Lee to the rear!" cried the men. "We will drive them back if General Lee will only go to the rear."

BELOW: Union corps commander John Sedgwick is brought down by a Confederate sharpshooter on May 9 during a battle around Spottsylvania Court-house.

LEFT: Some of the more than 2000 Confederate soldiers captured by the Federals at Spottsylvania on May 12.

ABOVE: The fight with Stuart's cavalry at Yellow Tavern. Here Jeb Stuart was mortally wounded. Of him, General Lee wrote, "A more zealous, ardent, brave, and devoted soldier than Stuart the Confederacy cannot have."

As Lee retired Gordon put himself at the head of his division and cried out in his ringing voice, "Forward! charge! and remember your promise to General Lee!"

The charge that followed was fierce and telling. . . . The works were retaken, the Confederate line again established, and an impending disaster converted into a brilliant victory.

During the 11th, General Grant was employed in shifting the positions of his corps preparatory to a new assault upon the Confederate lines. Before daylight on the morning of the 12th his army . . . was able to advance unobserved, to break through Johnson's line, and to capture his whole division. . . .

This success inaugurated one of the most desperate conflicts that occurred during the war. The long breach made by the capture of Johnson's division admitted the Federals in heavy masses. . . . From four o'clock in the morning until night the battle continued, marked by terrible slaughter. . . . At last the persistent attacks of the enemy were obliged

to yield to constant repulse and the Federals discontinued the contest.

*   *   *

The succession of bloody combats which had marked the career of Grant in the Wilderness had by this time so greatly reduced his army that he was obliged to pause and await reinforcements.

*   *   *

During the operations about Spottsylvania Court-house, Sheridan conceived the idea of capturing Richmond by a *coup de main*, and on the 9th proceeded to its execution. Of this movement General Stuart quickly became aware, and with his usual promptitude threw himself in Sheridan's path, and encountered him on the 10th at the Yellow Tavern, a few miles north of Richmond. A severe conflict ensued, in which Stuart fell mortally wounded, and his troops were compelled to retire before the superior numbers of the foe.

*   *   *

Sheridan had been so much delayed by Stuart's assault that the small force which had been left for the defence of Richmond had time to reach the works, which were very feebly garrisoned on Sheridan's first approach. He carried the first line, but recoiled from the second, and retired toward the Chickahominy.

* * *

No further effort was made by Grant on the desperately-fought field of Spottsylvania. Having been reinforced by 40,000 reserves, on the 20th of May he disappeared from the front of Lee's army. As in the Wilderness, he began a movement to turn the impregnable position of Spottsylvania by a flank march.

General Lee, however, with his usual alertness, had his men on the march the instant the movement of his adversary was discovered, and he advanced with such rapidity as to reach Hanover Junction, at the intersection of the Fredericksburg and Richmond and the Central railroads, in advance of Grant. This objective point of the Federal army was occupied by Lee on the 22nd. He at once took up a strong position, and when Grant arrived on the 23rd it was to find himself again intercepted by his active opponent.

* * *

General Grant on this occasion did not exhibit his usual pertinacity, but seemed satis-

BELOW: General Grant looking over General Meade's shoulder at a map during a war council outside Massaponnax Church on May 21, 1864.

fied by observation alone that the Confederate position could not be carried by main strength. He therefore proceeded down the North Anna to the Pamunkey, which he crossed on the 28th. . . .

* * *

Proceeding on his march from the Pamunkey, Grant found his advance upon Richmond again arrested by Lee, . . . Grant did not at this point attempt to force his opponent from his path, but moved slowly by his left flank toward the Chickahominy, while Lee, by a similar movement to his right, kept pace with him and constantly confronted him at every stage.

* * *

[By the first of June, the] old battlefield of Cold Harbor was again occupied by the contending forces, though in an inverse order.

The Confederate right now occupied the position that had been previously held by the Federals, and the Federal left held that which had been occupied by the Confederates. This field was about to become the theatre of a second conflict more desperate than the first.

Apparently with the intention of blotting out the memory of the defeat of the Federal arms on the former occasion, General Grant massed the flower of his army for battle. A portion of the Confederate line occupied the edge of a swamp of several hundred yards in length and breadth, enclosed by a low semi-circular ridge covered with brushwood. On the previous night the troops assigned to this part of the line, finding the ground wet and miry, withdrew to the encircling ridge, leaving the breastworks to be held by their picket-line. The attacking column quickly carried this part of the line, and advanced

BELOW: Union cavalry crossing Chesterfield Bridge over the North Anna River, moving toward the battlefield at Cold Harbor.

through the mud and water until arrested by the deliberate fire of the Confederates.

The battle that succeeded was one of the most desperately contested and murderous engagements of the war. Along the whole Federal line a simultaneous assault was made on the Confederate works, and at every point with the same disastrous result. Rank after rank was swept away until the column of assault was almost annihilated. Attack after attack was made, and men fell in myriads before the murderous fire from the Confederate line. While Hill, Breckenridge, Anderson, and Pickett repulsed Grant's desperate assaults upon the right, Early with Rodes, Gordon, and Ramseur on the left successfully opposed Burnside and Warren. In the brief space of one hour the bloody battle of the 3rd of June was over, and 13,000 dead and wounded Federals lay in front of the lines behind which little more than 1000 of the Confederate force had fallen.

A few hours afterward orders were sent to the corps commanders to renew the assault, and transmitted by them through the intermediate channels to the men. Then an event occurred which has seldom been witnessed on a battlefield, yet which testified most emphatically to the silent judgment of the men on the useless slaughter to which they had been subjected. Though the orders to advance were given, not a man stirred. The troops stood silent, but immovable, presenting in this unmistakable protest the verdict of the rank and file against the murderous work decided on by their commanders.

Thus ended Grant's overland campaign, in which his losses aggregated the enormous total of 60,000 men – a greater number than the whole of Lee's army at the beginning of the campaign. Lee's losses, on the contrary, were not more than 20,000. As to the *morale* of the two armies, that of Lee's continued excellent. Their successful defence against their powerful opponent had raised the spirits of the men and their confidence in their general to the highest pitch. On the contrary, the dreadful slaughter to which Grant's army had been subjected produced an inevitable sense of depression in the ranks, and a feeling that they were destined to destruction before the terrible blows of their able antagonist.

It is an error to suppose that in this campaign Lee was afraid to meet his adversary in open field, as had been asserted by Northern writers. He was always ready for action, whether offensive or defensive, under favorable circumstances. "I happen to know," says General Early, "that General Lee had always the greatest anxiety to strike at Grant in the open field." It was the practice of both armies, whenever encamping, to build intrenchments, and it would have been utter folly for Lee to leave his when he found his antagonist willing to attack him behind his breastworks, thus giving him that advantage of a defensive position which the smallness of his army imperatively demanded. Had he advanced against Grant, it would only have been to find the latter behind his works, and the comparative size of the two armies did

ABOVE: A. R. Waud's sketch of an artillery duel on June 2 at Cold Harbor.

139

ⁿ N.Y. Heavy Arty in Barlows charge, m Cold Harbor
Tuesday June 3rd 1864.

not warrant this reversal of the conditions of the contest.

At the beginning of the campaign, perceiving that General Grant's *rôle* was fighting and not manoeuvring, General Lee restrained his desire for the bold and adventurous offensive and strictly confined himself to the defensive, hoping in the course of events to reduce his opponent sufficiently near a physical equality to warrant his attacking him openly with reasonable hope of success. Believing that object had been accomplished after the battle of Cold Harbor, General Lee was anxious to assume the offensive and attack Grant before his army could recover from the stunning effect of its defeat on that occasion; but being obliged to send a large detachment from his army to oppose Sigel and Hunter in the Valley, he was compelled to continue on the defensive.

Grant, on his part, had been taught a costly lesson by his many bloody repulses, and after the battle of Cold Harbor changed his whole plan of operations, deciding to endeavor to accomplish by patient siege what he had failed to achieve by the reckless application of force. With this decision began a new chapter in the history of the war, and one of the most remarkable sieges known to history was inaugurated – that in which the Confederate commander behind the breastworks of Petersburg for a full year baffled every effort of his powerful foe.

* * *

OPPOSITE TOP: Engraving of a cavalry charge at Cold Harbor on June 1.

OPPOSITE BOTTOM: A fruitless assault by New York artillery on the Confederate position on June 3.

BELOW: Collecting remains for reburial long after the battle at Cold Harbor. In the last day's fighting, Grant lost some 13,000 killed and wounded, Lee about 1000.

Chapter VIII

The Siege of Petersburg

The war in Virginia [in 1864] had now been reduced to the attack and defence of Richmond – in other words, to a siege whose termination was only a question of time.

* * *

The battle of Cold Harbor had taught Grant the inutility and peril of direct assaults upon the Confederate intrenchments. He therefore determined upon siege operations, and about the middle of June he threw a large portion of his army south of the James and extended his line of investment so as to embrace the city of Petersburg. This caused Lee to make a counter-movement in order to cover that place and protect the rail-

roads leading to it. The capture of Petersburg was of primary importance to the Federals, as it would enable them to cut of two lines of communication very necessary for the support of Richmond, and at the same time to greatly contract their line of circumvallation. Therefore its possession was much desired.

* * *

General Grant, having failed in his various attempts to force the Confederate lines, acquiesced in a proposal to supplement the musket and the sabre with the spade and the pick. About the last of June it was proposed to mine and blow up a Confederate salient that was opposite to Burnside's position. At

BELOW: From mid-June 1864, the city of Petersburg, a rail center about 25 miles south of Richmond, was the focus of a Federal siege.

ABOVE: A railroad station near Petersburg. The city defied the Union siege for almost 10 months, until April 3, 1865.

that point the two lines were sufficiently near to warrant such an attempt. The conduct of this mining operation was assigned to the person by whom it had been originally proposed, Lieutenant-colonel Henry Pleasants of the Forty-eighth Pennsylvania, a skilful mining engineer. Pleasants found a suitable point to commence operations about five hundred feet distant from the salient to be blown up. His working-parties were drawn from his own regiment, which contained a number of experienced miners. The work was pushed forward so expeditiously that by the 23rd of July the mine was completed, and was charged with 8000 pounds of powder. The tamping was completed and the mine was pronounced ready for explosion by the 28th. It was decided that the mine should be sprung early on the morning of the 30th, and to that end the necessary preparations were made.

General Grant, in order to mask his real design, on the 26th sent Hancock and Sheridan with the Second corps and two divisions of cavalry to the north side of the James River, with instructions to threaten Lee's right, and thus to create the impression that a real attack was to be made in that quarter, while he perfected his arrangements for making the assault on Petersburg upon the explosion of the mine. At this time the Confederate force about Petersburg did not exceed 13,000 men, whilst opposed to this Grant had over 65,000. On the 29th were made the final dispositions for attack.

Hancock was directed on the night of the 29th to return from the north of the James with all secrecy and despatch, and to take part in the assault, while Sheridan was to pass in rear of the army and with his whole cavalry corps operate toward Petersburg from the south and west. On the evening of the 29th, Meade issued his orders of battle. As soon as it was dusk Burnside was to mass

his troops in front of the point to be attacked, and form there in columns of assault, taking care to remove the abatis, so that the troops could debouch rapidly, and to have his pioneers equipped for opening passages for the artillery. He was to spring the mine at 3.30 A.M., move rapidly through the breach, and seize the crest of Cemetery Hill, a ridge four hundred yards in rear of the Confederate lines.

Ord was to mass the Eighteenth corps in rear of the Ninth, immediately follow Burnside, and support him on the right. Warren was to reduce the number of men holding his front to the minimum, concentrate heavily on the right of his corps, and support Burnside on the left. Hancock was to mass the Second corps in rear of the trenches at that time held by Ord, and be prepared to support the assault as events might dictate.

Engineer officers were detailed to accompany each corps, and the chief engineer was directed to park his pontoon-train at a convenient point, ready to move at a moment's warning.

Meade having assured himself that the Confederates had no second line on Cemetery Hill, as he had formerly supposed and as Duane had positively reported, was now sanguine of success. He made these preparations to meet the contingency of the meagre Confederate force retiring beyond the Appomattox and burning the bridges; in which event he proposed to push immediately across that river to Swift Creek and open up communication with Butler at Bermuda Hundred, before Lee could send any reinforcements from his five divisions north of the James.

The commanders of the white divisions of Burnside's corps decided by lot which division should have the honor of making the assault, the chance favoring Ledlie's division, though, as the sequel shows, it had but little heart for . . . it.

On the morning of the 30th, shortly before the hour appointed for springing the mine, all the columns were in position ready for action. Half-past three arrived, but the silence of the morning was unbroken; minute after minute went by, while a painful suspense pervaded the expectant columns. Time passed on, yet silence continued to reign. The suspense became almost unbearable. The delay could not be understood, and various conjectures flew rapidly among the troops. At last it was discovered that the fuse had gone out within fifty yards of the mine.

All this time the Confederates lay in

OPPOSITE TOP: Men of the 48th Pennsylvania carrying powder to the mine.

OPPOSITE BOTTOM: Soldiers from Colonel Pleasants's regiment digging the tunnel toward the Confederate salient.

BELOW: Union soldiers in the trenches before Petersburg.

peaceful slumber, unconscious of the terrible storm that was about to burst upon them. The fuse was relighted, and at about half-past four the flame reached the powder in the mine.

A tremendous explosion instantly followed, and there was hurled into the air an immense column of smoke and earth, which, after rising to a great height, burst into fragments of timber, stone, broken guncarriages, muskets, and black and mutilated corpses, which quickly returned in a heavy shower upon the earth. Two hundred men were killed by the explosion, and a rent was torn in the Confederate lines 135 feet long, 90 feet wide, and 30 feet deep.

The whole Confederate line was aroused by the explosion. The men in the immediate vicinity of the line were for some minutes paralyzed by the shock, while those on the more distant portions of the lines remained a while in a state of ignorance and wonder as to what had occurred.

But the troops stationed near the mine soon became conscious of the catastrophe, and, alive to the importance of immediate action, Lieutenant-colonel John Haskell, who commanded the artillery at that point, turned his guns upon the approaches to the breach, and poured such a destructive fire of canister and shell upon them as to render the advance of the enemy extremely diffi-

BELOW: The explosion of the mine under Confederate defenses on July 30. General Grant lost 5000 men in the ensuing disaster.

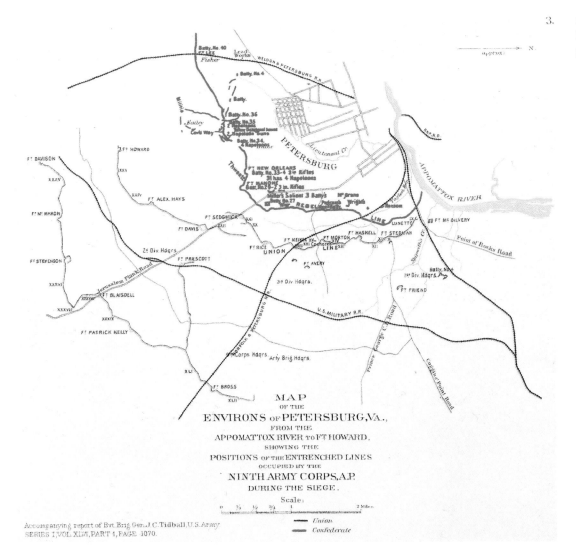

cult. Some time elapsed before the assaulting column could be got in motion, and when it cleared the breastwork it was met by such a storm of shot and shell that it was thrown into confusion, and the men were so demoralized that they hastily sought shelter. Great numbers rushed into the crater of the mine; others hid themselves behind traverses; some even crouched close beneath the Confederate breastworks, and no efforts of their officers could induce them to advance. The delay thus occasioned enabled the Confederates to collect a force sufficient to defend the breach.

General Lee, who had been early apprised of the disaster, sent Colonel Venable of his staff to hasten forward troops from other parts of the line. This energetic officer first found General Mahone, whose division was already under arms, and instructed him to proceed to the threatened point. Mahone rapidly advanced, and on reaching the crater promptly formed a cordon of bayonets and took decisive steps to expel the Federal forces that had effected a lodgment upon the Confederate works. Mahone's

forces were rapidly reinforced by other troops, and the fighting now became desperate. The Federals, who had for some time been delayed, pushed forward with great resolution and with the determination to counteract the effects of the blunder that had been made in the first assault. But all their efforts were unavailing, and by ten o'clock they were driven back within their own lines.

The mine, instead of opening the gate to victory, had proved a sepulchre. General Grant lost 5000 men in his attempt to pass the breach. Although the distance between the hostile breastworks was barely a hundred yards, only a few of the Federals succeeded in establishing on the Confederate works. The only advantage to the Federals was in the blowing up of 200 Confederates and the killing and wounding of a few hundreds more. The men thus lost by the Confederates could never be replaced, and to this extent General Grant saw himself a step nearer the end.

Generals Lee and Beauregard were eye-witnesses of the gallant defence of the

ABOVE: Confederate General P. G. T. Beauregard commanded the 50,000 defenders of Petersburg until Lee's arrival on June 18.

RIGHT: Colonel David Weisiger led the brigade that repelled the attackers from the crater.

breach and the signal repulse of the enemy. Colonel Weisiger, whose brigade encircled the crater, repelled the enemy with great determination, and his gallantry won for him the grade of brigadier-general. Captain Girardey, for his gallant conduct, received a similar promotion, while the names of Lieutenant-colonels John Haskell, Pegram, and many others of the artillery obtained prominence in the roll of honor.

Critical remarks in reference to the strategic bearings of this mining operation are perhaps uncalled for. The mine itself proved useless and became a death-trap to its excavators; yet, if we accept the Federal statements, this was a result of bad management after the explosion, and has no necessary bearing on the question of the military value of the undertaking itself. To mine fortified works which cannot be breached or scaled has long been a common expedient in siege operations, but to attack an earthwork by such a method had never before been attempted, and its ill-success on this occasion will probably prevent its being quickly again essayed.

Federal historians and military authorities ascribe the non-success of the enterprise to an unwise withdrawal, at the last moment, of the black troops, who had been carefully drilled for this special service, and their replacement by a brigade of whites, who were very badly led and held back from charging until the Confederates in the vicinity had recovered from their temporary panic and had hastened to the defence of their imperilled lines. Yet this censure of General Ledlie seems hardly just in view of all the circumstances of the case. The crater into which its division plunged was very difficult to pass – much more so than an ordinary earthwork. And the lack of previous training of his men, or of any full comprehension on his part of the character of the work before him, operated as a serious disadvantage. Had men trained to the work been given the advance in the charge, the result might possibly have been very different. It cannot be denied that the Confederate position was for a short time in serious jeopardy, and that had the Federals taken instant and decided advantage of their opportunity they might have gained an important victory. There has seldom been a case in which the old adage, "Delay is dangerous," more fully applied, yet it was one of those cases in which delay is almost unavoidable, and it becomes a question, therefore, whether there was suffi-

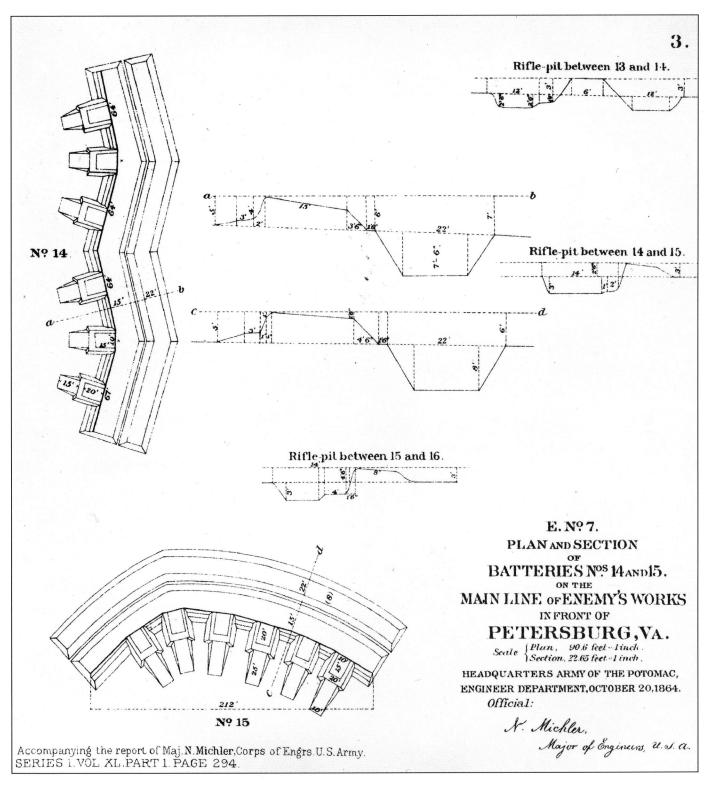

3.

Rifle-pit between 13 and 14.

NO 14.

Rifle-pit between 14 and 15.

Rifle-pit between 15 and 16.

E. NO 7.
PLAN AND SECTION
OF
BATTERIES NOS 14 AND 15.
ON THE
MAIN LINE OF ENEMY'S WORKS
IN FRONT OF
PETERSBURG, VA.
Scale { Plan, 90.6 feet=1 inch.
{ Section, 22.65 feet=1 inch.
HEADQUARTERS ARMY OF THE POTOMAC,
ENGINEER DEPARTMENT, OCTOBER 20, 1864.
Official:

N. Michler,
Major of Engineers, U.S.A.

NO 15

Accompanying the report of Maj. N. Michler, Corps of Engrs. U.S. Army.
SERIES 1. VOL XL. PART 1. PAGE 294.

cient probability of success to warrant such a dangerous enterprise.

* * *

After the failure of the mining enterprise direct assaults flagged, and during the remainder of the summer and the autumn the spade took the place of the musket, and both armies employed themselves in constructing new and strengthening old works.

* * *

Large detachments which had been with-drawn from Grant's army, first to oppose Early, and subsequently for [an] expedition against Wilmington, had so reduced his force as to prevent very vigorous operations against Richmond and Petersburg. [He spent the winter of 1864-1865 in rebuilding his army for a final assault on Lee's defenses. (Ed)]

In the mean time, Lee, finding himself too weak to hazard a serious blow, did all he could to preserve his army from the constant attrition that was wearing it away. . . .

* * *

ABOVE: Army of the Potomac engineers drew these plans of Confederate batteries and rifle pits in front of Petersburg.

Right Section. Comp. E. 3rd N.Y. Art.y. Capt. Ashby. 20 pounder parrots.

During this period, on February 6, 1865, [General Lee was appointed] commander-in-chief of all the Confederate armies. Had this appointment been made two years earlier, it is probable that a different state of affairs would have existed. . . . But as the spring opened it became daily more apparent that human power and endurance could do no more, and that a forced evacuation of the beleaguered cities was near at hand.

*   *   *

Grant had begun the concentration of his forces in order to complete his interior cordon or line of investment. . . . While his adversary was thus active, Lee was not idle. He had formed a plan to surprise the enemy's centre by a night-attack, which if successful would have given him possession of a commanding position in the enemy's rear and control of the military railroad to City Point – a very important part of Grant's communications.

*   *   *

Now was the time for the supporting column to advance. . . . For some reason which has never been made very clear this advance was not made. . . . Gordon with his small force was left to bear the whole brunt of the Federal assault which quickly fell upon him. . . .

This unsuccessful effort was quickly followed by a vigorous advance on the part of Grant, who concentrated his principal force south and west of Petersburg with the view of assailing the Confederate right. Early on the morning of March 29th the corps of Warren and Humphreys broke camp and moved toward Lee's intrenchments on the extreme right, while Sheridan, with the cavalry, made a wider sweep and occupied Dinwiddie Court-house, six miles south-west of the point reached by the infantry.

Yet, swiftly and secretly as this movement was made, it did not escape Lee's vigilant eye. He quickly divined where the blow was to fall, and, leaving the works north of the James under Longstreet and those at Petersburg under Gordon but weakly garrisoned, he removed the remainder of his army, con-

ABOVE: This Confederate soldier died on April 2, 1865, the day General Lee finally evacuated his position and led his troops out of Petersburg.

OPPOSITE TOP: A battery of the 3rd New York Artillery in the trenches before Petersburg.

OPPOSITE BOTTOM: A section of the trenches, which would be occupied by soldiers for almost 10 months.

RIGHT: Fort Sedgwick, on the Plank Road opposite the center of Lee's Petersburg defenses, formed part of General Grant's siege line.

OPPOSITE: Part of the Union arsenal at City Point, Virginia, in 1864 demonstrates the depth of Federal power.

BELOW: The harbor at City Point is filled with ships from the industrial North unloading supplies for Grant's army in Virginia.

sisting of about 15,000 infantry and 2000 cavalry, into the works along the White Oak road.

Here, on the morning of the 31st, Lee made the flank attack which he had so often attempted with success against the Federal columns. Not waiting for the assault, he boldly took the initiative, and fell upon their exposed flank while they were entangled in the intricacies of a swampy forest. So sudden and heavy was the blow that the divisions encountered hastily gave way. But upon meeting the main body of the Federal troops he found it so thickly massed and well posted as to render an assault hopeless. He therefore fell back to his works.

On the same day Sheridan advanced toward Five Forks. Before reaching that point, however, he was encountered by the Confederate cavalry under the chief command of General Fitz Lee, supported by the infantry under Pickett. A severe combat ensued, in which Sheridan was driven back to Dinwiddie Court-house. . . .

On the 1st of April, Sheridan was reinforced by two corps of infantry, and with this powerful aid he renewed his attack upon Five Forks, which place was carried late in the evening and the Confederates driven back.

General Lee, perceiving that his forces were too weak to combat successfully with the enemy, ordered Longstreet on the afternoon of the 1st to bring his corps with all speed from before Richmond to Petersburg, with the object of supporting his right wing.

Early on the morning of the 2nd the Federals renewed the attack, breaking the lines of the Confederates and forcing them from their position. The Federals then took possession of the Southside Railroad with little opposition, while the Confederates fell back toward Petersburg, followed by the victorious enemy. The pursuit was continued until it was arrested by the guns from two redoubts, Forts Alexander and Gregg, which with great gallantry held the enemy in check until Longstreet came up and interposed his corps, effectually arresting the further advance of the Federal columns.

In the conflict here described fell many gallant warriors, chief among them Lieutenant-general A. P. Hill, who was slain while endeavoring to reach Heth's division, which had been ordered to support Pickett on the right. No man had been more distinguished throughout the war for chivalric bearing than this brave soldier. On every field where appeared the Army of Northern Virginia he had borne a conspicuous part, and now in the last battle of that noble army he found a hero's grave.

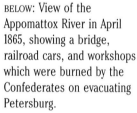

BELOW: View of the Appomattox River in April 1865, showing a bridge, railroad cars, and workshops which were burned by the Confederates on evacuating Petersburg.

ABOVE: A Confederate soldier lies dead at Fort Mahone after the evacuation of Petersburg.

LEFT: The occupation of the Petersburg defenses by Union troops on April 2, 1865.

Chapter IX

Appomattox

The success of the Federal army in breaking the lines of Petersburg had rendered the retreat of the Confederate force imperative. . . . But by abandoning his works and concentrating his army, which still amounted to about 30,000 men, General Lee might retire to some natural stronghold in the interior, where the defensible features of the country would enable him to oppose Grant's formidable host until he could rally strength to strike an effective blow.

* * *

Along the north bank of the Appomattox moved the long lines of artillery and dark columns of infantry through the . . . night [of April 2nd], over the roads leading to Amelia Court-house. By midnight the evacuation was completed. . . .

* * *

The retreat of Lee's army did not long remain unknown to the Federals . . . and they lost no time in taking possession of the abandoned works and entering the defenceless cities. On the morning of the 3rd of April the mayor of Richmond surrendered the city to the Federal commander in its vicinity. . . .

As soon as Grant became aware of Lee's line of retreat he pushed forward his whole available force . . . in order to intercept him on the line of the Richmond and Danville Railroad. . . . Lee pressed on as rapidly as possible to Amelia Court-house, where he had ordered supplies to be deposited for the use of his troops on their arrival. . . . Through an unfortunate error . . . not a single ration was found to be provided for the hungry troops. . . . The only chance remaining to the Army of Northern Virginia was to reach the hill-country without delay. . . . By the morning of the 5th the whole army had

BELOW: Federal columns moving on Richmond. On April 2 whole sections of the Confederate capital were burned by troops preparing to abandon it to the approaching Federals.

ABOVE: The evacuation of Richmond. Nearly one thousand buildings were destroyed in the fires, and many were damaged.

LEFT: Federal troops entered Richmond on April 3, and raised the Stars and Stripes over the Southern Capitol that morning. Mrs. Robert E. Lee remained in the city under protective guard.

RIGHT: Union soldiers survey
the ruins of occupied
Richmond.

reached the place of general rendezvous. Bitter was its disappointment to learn that no food was to be had. . . .

*   *   *

Sheridan's cavalry was already upon the flank of the Confederate army, and the infantry was following with all speed. On [the afternoon of the 6th]. . . . Ewell's, the rearmost corps in the army, closed upon those in front at a position on Sailor's Creek, a small tributary of the Appomattox River . . . [but] his corps was surrounded by the pursuing columns and captured with but little opposition. About the same time the divisions of Anderson, Pickett, and Bushrod Johnson were almost broken up, about 10,000 men in all being captured. The remainder of the army continued its retreat during the night of the 6th, and reached Farmville early on the morning of the 7th, where the troops obtained two days' rations. . . .

*   *   *

The heads of the Federal columns beginning to appear about eleven o'clock, the Confederates resumed their retreat. The teams of the wagons and artillery were weak, being travel worn and suffering from lack of forage. Their progress, therefore, was necessarily slow, and as the troops were obliged to move in conformity with the artillery and trains, the Federal cavalry closed upon the retreating army. . . .

*   *   *

Desperate as the situation had become, and irretrievable as it seemed hourly growing, General Lee could not forego the hope of breaking through the net that was rapidly enclosing him and of forming a junction with Johnston. In the event of success in this he felt confident of being able to manoeuvre with Grant at least until favorable terms of peace could be obtained. . . .

On the 8th the retreat, being uninterrupted, progressed more expeditiously than on the previous day. Yet, though the Federals did not press the Confederate flank and rear as on the day before, a heavy column of cavalry advanced upon Appomattox Station, where the supplies for the Confederate army had been deposited. . . . When Lee in the afternoon reached the neighborhood of Appomattox Court-house, he was met by the intelligence of the capture of the stores placed for his army. . . .

RIGHT: Jubilant Union soldiers
pose for a photo at
Appomattox Court-house.

On the evening of that day the last council of the leaders of the Army of Northern Virginia was held around a bivouac-fire in the woods, there being present Generals Lee, Longstreet, Gordon, and Fitz Lee. This conference ended in a determination to make a renewed effort on the following morning to break through the impediments in front. . . . At three o'clock on the morning of the 9th of April the Confederates moved silently forward.

* * *

Colonel C. S. Venable of General Lee's staff graphically tells what took place at

headquarters on that eventful morning. His story is of great interest, as showing how reluctantly yet how nobly the heroic commander submitted to the inevitable after having till the last minute, like a lion at bay, faced the overwhelming force of his opponent:

At three o'clock on the morning of that fatal day General Lee rode forward, still hoping that we might break through the countless hordes of the enemy who hemmed us in. Halting a short distance in rear of our vanguard, he sent me on to General Gordon to ask him if he could break through the enemy. I found General Gordon and General

BELOW: The McLean House at Appomattox Court-house, where Grant and Lee agreed upon the terms of surrender on April 9.

Fitz Lee on their front line in the dim light of the morning arranging an attack. Gordon's reply to the message (I give the expressive phrase of the gallant Georgian) was this: "Tell General Lee I have fought my corps to a frazzle, and I fear I can do nothing unless I am heavily supported by Longstreet's corps."

When I bore this message back to General Lee he said, "Then there is nothing left me but to go and see General Grant, and I would rather die a thousand deaths."

Convulsed with passionate grief, many were the wild words which we spoke as we stood around him. Said one, "Oh, general, what will history say of the surrender of the army in the field?"

He replied, "Yes, I know they will say hard things of us: they will not understand how we were overwhelmed by numbers. But that is not the question, colonel: the question is, Is it right to surrender this army? If it is right, then *I* will take *all* the responsibility."

The artillery had been withdrawn from the heights, as above stated, and parked in the small valley east of the village, while the infantry, who were formed on the left, stacked arms and silently waited the result of the interview between the opposing commanders.

The flag of truce was sent out from General Gordon's lines. Grant had not yet come up, and while waiting for his arrival General Lee seated himself upon some rails which Colonel Talcott of the Engineers had

ABOVE: Ulysses S. Grant and two of his staff. Grant's surrender terms were simple and generous.

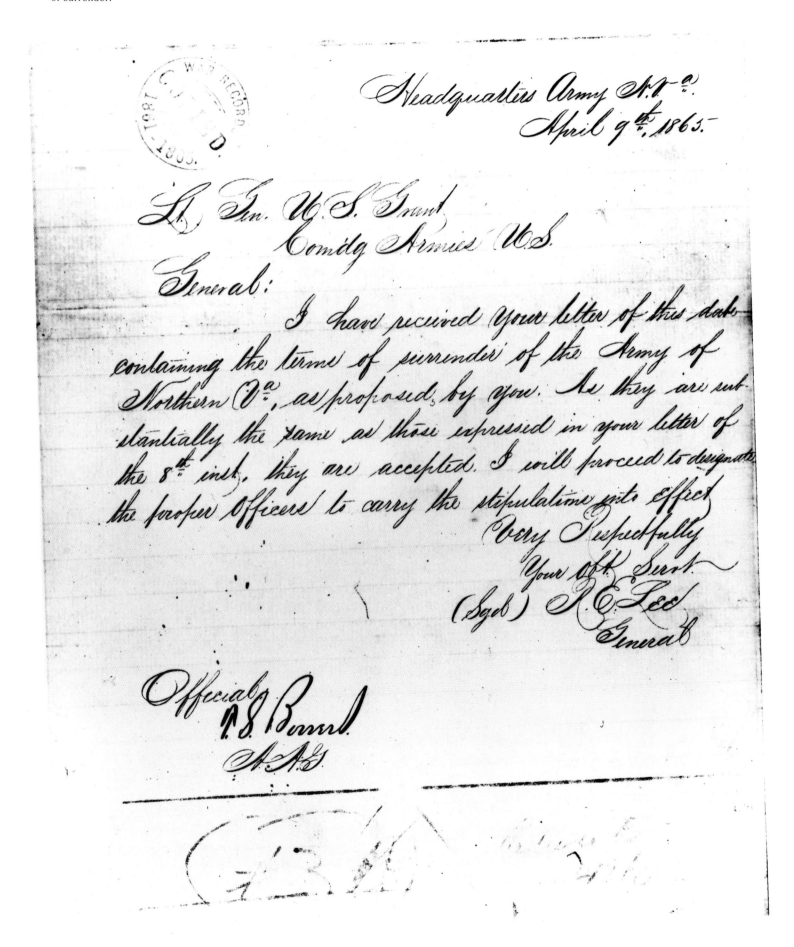

BELOW: Inscribed with part of a quotation from Lee, "Peace, the Sole object of All," and with the words, "Truce –then Peace," Thomas Nast's evocative, bold sketch of the defeated commander captures Lee's solid nobility.

fixed at the foot of an apple tree for his convenience. This tree was half a mile distant from the point where the meeting of Lee and Grant took place, yet widespread currency has been given to the story that the surrender took place under its shade, and "apple-tree" jewelry has been profusely distributed from the orchard in which it grew.

About 11 o'clock General Lee, accompanied only by Colonel Marshall of his staff, proceeded to the village to meet General Grant, who had now arrived. The meeting between the two renowned generals took place at the house of a Mr. McLean at Appomattox Court-house, to which mansion, after exchanging courteous salutations, they repaired to settle the terms on which the surrender of the Army of Northern Virginia should be concluded.

A conversation here took place which General Grant, as he himself tells us, led to various subjects divergent from the immediate purpose of the meeting, talking of old army matters and comparing recollections with General Lee. As he says, the conversation grew so pleasant that he almost forgot the object of the meeting.

GENERAL R. E. LEE'S
FAREWELL ADDRESS
APRIL 10th 1865

After four years of arduous service, marked by unsurpassed courage and fortitude, the Army of Northern Virginia has been compelled to yield to overwhelming numbers and resources. I need not tell the brave survivors of so many hard-fought battles, who have remained steadfast to the last, that I have consented to this result from no distrust of them; but feeling that valor and devotion could accomplish nothing that would compensate for the loss that must have attended a continuance of the contest, I determined to avoid the useless sacrifice of those whose past services have endeared them to their countrymen. By the terms of agreement officers and men can return to their homes and remain until exchanged. You will take with you the satisfaction that proceeds from the consciousness of duty faithfully performed, and I earnestly pray that a merciful God will extend to you His blessing and protection. With an increasing admiration of your constancy and devotion to your country and a grateful remembrance of your kind and generous consideration of myself, I bid you all an affectionate farewell.

APRIL 10th, 1865.

STRATFORD HOUSE, VIRGINIA, BIRTHPLACE OF LEE.

LEE CHAPEL, VIRGINIA, BENEATH WHICH THE GENERAL WAS BURIED.

General Lee was obliged more than once to remind him of this object, and it was some time before the terms of the surrender were written out. The written instrument of surrender covered the following points: Duplicate rolls of all the officers and men were to be made, and the officers to sign paroles for themselves and their men, all agreeing not to bear arms against the United States unless regularly exchanged. The arms, artillery, and public property were to be turned over to an officer appointed to receive them, the officers retaining their side-arms and private horses and baggage. In addition to this, General Grant permitted every man of the Confederate army who claimed to own a horse or mule to retain it for farming purposes, General Lee remarking that this would have a happy effect. As for the surrender by General Lee of his sword, a report of what has been widely circulated, General Grant disposes of it in the following words: "The much-talked of surrendering of Lee's sword and my handing it back, this and much more that has been said about it is the purest romance."

After completion of these measures General Lee remarked that his men were badly in need of food, that they had been living for several days on parched corn exclusively, and requested rations and forage for 25,000 men. These rations were granted out of the car-loads of Confederate provisions which had been stopped by the Federal cavalry. As for forage, Grant remarked that he was himself depending upon the country for that. The negotiations completed, General Lee left the house, mounted his horse, and rode back to headquarters.

It is impossible to describe the anguish of the troops when it was known that the surrender of the army was inevitable. Of all their trials, this was the greatest and hardest to endure. There was no consciousness of shame; each heart could boast with honest pride that its duty had been done to the end, and that still unsullied remained its honor. When, after his interview with Grant, General Lee again appeared, a shout of welcome instinctively ran through the army. But instantly recollecting the sad occasion that brought him before them, their shouts sank into silence, every hat was raised, and the bronzed faces of the thousands of grim warriors were bathed with tears.

As he rode slowly along the lines hundreds of his devoted veterans pressed around the noble chief, trying to take his hand, touch his person, or even lay a hand upon his horse, thus exhibiting for him their great affection. The general then, with head bare and tears flowing freely down his manly cheeks, bade adieu to the army. In a few words he told the brave men who had been so true in arms to return to their homes and become worthy citizens.

Thus closed the career of the noble Army of Northern Virginia.

OPPOSITE: General Robert E. Lee's April 10 farewell to the men of the Army of Northern Virginia.

LEFT: General Lee, mounted on his famous horse Traveller, returning to his veterans after the surrender to General Grant. The sketch is probably by the artist A. R. Waud.

BELOW: General Lee's farewell to his soldiers.

Chapter X

General Lee as a Soldier

With the surrender of the Army of Northern Virginia, General Lee's military career ended. My intimate relations with him continued to the close of his life.

I frequently visited him at his home in Lexington, Va., and saw him in the discharge of his duties as a college president, but before laying aside my pen it is proper that I should attempt some estimate of him as a soldier and a man.

General Lee was both by nature and by education a great soldier. By diligent study under the most favorable conditions, and by long and varied experience, he became a master of the science of war in all its branches. In early life he was especially distinguished as an engineer. All the important points from the coast of Georgia to New York bear witness to his engineering skill, and his name will be identified with the Rip Raps, Fort Carroll, and the defences of New York

BELOW: The famous postwar photo of General Robert E. Lee and his horse Traveller, taken in September 1866.

Gen's R. E. LEE and J. E. JOHNSTON.

D. J. Ryan,   Savannah, Ga.

BELOW: General Lee with
General Joseph E. Johnston
in a photo taken about 1870,
the year of Lee's death.

harbor until those granite structures crumble into dust.

Perhaps even more important than his work on the Atlantic coast was that on the Mississippi and Des Moines rapids, of which General Meigs, U. S. A., has kindly furnished for this volume a highly interesting account.

The Mexican War opened to him a wider field, and the quick eye of General Scott discovered in the young captain of Engineers "a man of all kinds of merit."

On assuming command in Virginia in April, 1861, General Lee once showed his talents for administration and organization. He found the country almost destitute of the essentials of war, and, as if by magic, he created and equipped an army. His very ability as an organizer made many doubt whether he could be great in other directions, and it was only after successful trial that they were willing to recognize his wonderful versatility.

It was with surprise that they saw him showing himself equal to all the demands made upon him as the commander of a great army in the field. As they looked on, their surprise changed to admiration; the glory of the engineer and organizer was first dimmed, and then eclipsed, by that of the strategist and tactician.

The great soldier is something more than a fighter of battles. He must have a breadth of view sufficient to take in widely-separated movements and to form great and far-reaching combinations. That General Lee had this breadth of view, this subtle intuition, which constitutes the very flower of military genius, is shown by the whole history of the war. The reader will recall how, when he was contemplating an attack on McClellan on the Chickahominy, he sent Jackson to make a vigorous movement in the Valley. He nicely calculated the moral effect of that movement. He intended it to alarm the authorities at Washington – to hold McDowell in position near the Federal capital, and thus prevent his joining in the coming battle.

The Pennsylvania campaign had a wider outlook: it was charged with great possibilities. The defeat of Meade's army in Pennsylvania might be expected to be much more than the simple defeat of that one army. Its effect would be felt on the Mississippi; Grant's army would be needed in the East; the siege of Vicksburg would be raised, and Pemberton's army released for active service. What else might follow it was easy to conjecture. Lee fought, and knew that he

ABOVE: A Confederate soldier of Company A, 18th Virginia Infantry, in dress uniform.

Ridge for a while seemed successful, then the Muse of History took up her pen to record the birth of a new nation.

Breadth of plan is often neutralized by neglect of details. General Lee did not make that mistake. Before a battle he neglected nothing that might be needful either for attack or defence; in the battle he was quick to see and prompt to meet emergencies. He knew his men, rank and file – what they could do, and how far he might trust them. He was careful to know the ground on which he was to operate, and also to seize and use every advantage of position: he made a league with rivers and mountains and mountain-passes. He studied his adversary, knew his peculiarities, and adapted himself to them. His own methods no one could foresee; he varied them with every change in the commanders opposed to him. He had one method with McClellan, another with Pope, another with Hooker, and yet another with Grant. But for a knowledge of his own resources, of the field, and of his adversary some of his movements might have been rash. As it was, they were wisely bold. Because he was so attentive to details, and guarded so rigidly against the accidents of battle, he was sometimes supposed to be over-cautious; because he sometimes supposed to be over-cautious; because he sometimes attacked greatly superior numbers or divided his forces, he was often thought over-bold. The truth is, that there was in him that harmonious blending of caution and boldness without which a general must often either rashly expose himself to defeat or lose an opportunity for victory.

Whatever other qualities a man may have, he cannot be a great soldier unless he has the power to win the confidence and inspire the enthusiasm of his men. General Lee had this power; few men have had it in a higher degree. No privation or suffering or disaster could shake the confidence of his men in him. In the darkest hour the sight of his form or the mention of his name stirred the hearts of his veterans. They spoke of him with an affection and pride that have not been dimmed by the lapse of years.

It is sometimes said that while General Lee was without a peer in defence, he was not so great in attack. That he was great in defence is witnessed by the series of combats from the Wilderness to Cold Harbor. Hardly anything in the history of warfare, ancient or modern, equals the skill and

fought, for a great stake. That he did not succeed and that the movement came too late, even if it had been successful, to affect the result at Vicksburg, detracts nothing from the brilliancy of the conception. The one pertinent thing is that the Confederate general saw that by a single bold and successful stroke it might be possible virtually to end the war and secure the independence of the Southern Confederacy. That success was possible is shown by the narrow chance by which it failed. It has been well said that when the Confederate charge at Cemetery

Great Seal of the
Confederate States of
America.

LEFT: An engraving of notable
Confederate generals. At
center, Stonewall Jackson;
clockwise from top, Jeb
Stuart, Leonidas Polk, John
B. Magruder, A. P. Hill, James
Longstreet, R. S. Ewell, John
Pemberton, and Sterling
Price.

RIGHT: Confederate President
Jefferson Davis surrounded
by his senior officers.
Clockwise from top, P. T. G.
Beauregard, Robert E. Lee,
Braxton Bragg, G. N. Hollins,
Simon B. Buckner, A. S.
Johnston, and Joseph E.
Johnston.

adroitness with which he met and repulsed Grant's obstinate and persevering assaults. But, on the other hand, in the second battle of Manassas and at Chancellorsville he was the aggressor; he went to seek the enemy. And even in those cases in which he was resisting the enemy's advance he often struck a blow in preference to waiting to receive one.

But perhaps the readiest way to fix Lee's position and to realize his greatness would be to compare him with others. It is significant that in attempting to do this no one ever thinks of comparing him with any but men of the first rank. Among the distinguished soldiers on the Confederate side his position was peculiar. He came from the old army with a brilliant reputation, and during the war he occupied the most prominent and responsible position. It is no injustice either to

the living or the dead to say that by common consent he holds the first place among Southern soldiers.

Among the dead heroes of the war Albert Sidney Johnston challenges admiring attention. He had great qualities; anything that skill, courage, and a lofty, unselfish character might accomplish seemed possible to him; but he died at Shiloh. Jackson was Lee's most trusted lieutenant, and deserved all the confidence that his commander reposed in him. In the sphere of his operations he had no superior, nor can it be known that he would not have shown himself equal to a greater sphere. All honor to that brave, true soldier! but it would not be proper to compare him with his chief. There was no rivalry between them living; let there be none now that they are dead. There was A. P. Hill, a modest man, always ready; one of the finest soldiers in the army: he had the best division when he had a division, and one of the best corps when he had a corps. Lee and Jackson agreed in their admiration of Hill, and both mentioned him in the delirium of death; but no one thinks of comparing him with Lee.

There is a sort of infallibility in an undivided popular judgment, and the whole South looked to Lee as its greatest man. So impressed was Grant with the devotion of

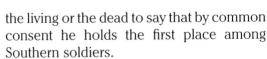

ABOVE LEFT: Engraving of General Stonewall Jackson.

ABOVE: Photographic portrait of General Jackson.

the Southern people to Lee that after the surrender at Appomattox he sought his influence, being convinced that if he should advise the surrender of all the Southern armies, the advice would be followed with alacrity. And in his report of the operations of the Army of the Potomac in 1864-65 he attributes it to General Lee's example that, as he says, "the armies lately under his leadership are at their homes, desiring peace and quiet, and their arms are in the hands of our ordnance officers."

Nothing is more characteristic of General Lee, or reveals more clearly his simple moral grandeur, than the fact that when no more could be accomplished by arms he used his influence to promote peace and good feeling toward the people against whom he had been waging war.

Of the great soldiers opposed to General Lee, some may have equalled him in single qualities, none in the combination of qualities. They were great in some directions; he in many. Let it not be forgotten that his was a

long and varied career, and that he was distinguished in every part of it. He was called on to do many things, and he did them all in a masterly way.

In judging him account must be taken not only of what he did in the war between the States, but also of what he did before the Mexican War, in the Mexican War, and after the Mexican War, and in the last years of his life. When all these things are considered, and when we take into the account his perfect acquaintance with his art, his organizing power, his skill in combining, his wisdom in planning, his boldness and vigor in execution, his power to awaken enthusiasm and to lead men, we must place him first among the great soldiers of both armies. The time has not yet come to compare him with soldiers of the past and of other lands. They show great in the haze of time and distance, but the time will come when by the suffrages of all he will take his place among the greatest of those who have marshalled armies to battle.

OPPOSITE: Sketch by A. R. Waud of the railroad bridge over the Rappannock at Fredericksburg. Burned before the Union attack, it became a place where men of both sides came to exchange jibes.

BELOW: Men of the Union VI Corps fighting in the woods at the Battle of the Wilderness.

OPPOSITE: Ruins of the city of Richmond in April 1865.

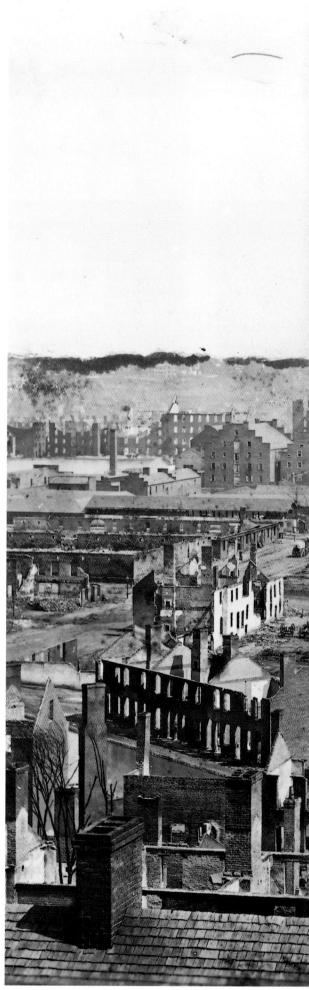

We turn now from Lee as a soldier to Lee as a man; and here it is difficult to find suitable words in which to speak of him. In a private conversation a gentleman once said to an officer who had been intimately associated with him, "Most men have their weak point. What was General Lee's?" After a thoughtful pause, the answer was, "I really do not know." This answer may be taken for that of the great majority of those who knew him personally or who have studied his character. He was singularly free from the faults which so often mar the character of great men. He was without envy, jealousy, or suspicion, self-seeking, or covetousness; there was nothing about him to diminish or chill the respect which all men felt for him. General Grant speaks of him as "a large, austere man, difficult of approach to his subordinates." "Austere" is not the word to use in speaking of him. I should rather say that he was clothed with a natural dignity which could either repel or invite as occasion might require. He could pass with perfect ease from familiar, cheerful conversation to earnest conference, and from earnest conference to authoritative command. He had a pleasant humor, could see the ludicrous side of things, and could enjoy an anecdote or a joke. But even in his lightest moods he was still the cultivated gentleman, having that just degree of reserve that suited his high and responsible position.

His character was perfectly simple; there were in it no folds or sinuosities. It was simple because guided by a single principle. It is common to say that this principle was duty. This is not the whole truth. Duty is faithfulness to obligation, and is measured by obligation. That which moulded General

BELOW: Confederate soldiers withdraw after the Battle of Gettysburg.

ABOVE: The state house at Richmond rises above the ruins of the business district.

Lee's life was something more than duty. It was a fine soldierly instinct that made him feel that it was his business to devote his life and powers to the accomplishment of high impersonal ends. Duty is the highest conception of Roman stoicism; it was the ambition of the Christian soldier to serve. General Grant interpreted him correctly when he said, "I knew there was no use to urge him to anything against his ideas of right."

If there are any who blame him for resigning his position in the United States army and taking part with the South, they must at the same time acknowledge that he was influenced by no unworthy motive. What he did involved sacrifice of feeling, or position, and of interest: he might have had the highest place in the old army; he had but to consent to take it. A man of smaller mould might have been dazzled and attracted by the prospect of leading a successful revolution and establishing a new nation, but in all my association with him I saw no indication that any feeling of personal ambition was present with him. If he had such feeling it was checked by a consciousness of the great interests confided to him.

As he appeared to me, so he appeared to others. When the Confederate capital was transferred from Montgomery to Richmond, the Virginia forces, of which he was commander-in-chief, were incorporated in the Confederate army. He then lost his independent command. While the transfer was yet in contemplation the Confederate authorities were anxious to know whether an apparent lowering of his rank would offend to make him less zealous in the service of the Confederacy. When Mr. Stephens, the Confederate Vice-President, mentioned the matter to him, he promptly said, "Mr. Stephens, I am willing to serve anywhere where I can be useful."

It was in perfect accord with his character that he was no stickler for rank or position. In the early part of the war the positions held by him were not such as to attract public attention; the duties assigned to him, while very important, were not of a showy kind. Others were winning distinction in the field and rising into prominence, while he was in the background. No great laurels could be won in the mountains of West Virginia or in strengthening the coast defences of South Carolina and Georgia. In the estimation of the general public his reputation was suffering; it was said that his former distinction had been too easily won. During this time he uttered no word of complaint, and gave no intimation that he felt himself in any way wronged or overlooked. One might wonder whether this sweetness of spirit, this calmness, this cheerful content, did not spring from a consciousness of power and assured belief that he had only to bide his time; but a close acquaintance with the workings of his mind convinced me that it was rather from a single-hearted desire to be useful, and the conviction that the best way to be useful was to work contentedly and to the best of his ability in the place assigned him.

It was his constant feeling that he was living and working to an end that constituted the source of General Lee's magnanimity and put him far above any petty jealousy. He looked at everything as unrelated to himself,

BELOW: Confederate soldiers of Company B, 9th Mississippi Infantry, camped at Warrington Navy Yard, Pensacola, Florida.

ABOVE: Music cover for the Confederate anthem "God Save the South."

RIGHT: Union soldiers at the west end of Arlington House, Lee's former residence. The grounds of the house became Arlington National Cemetery.

and only as it affected the cause he was serving. This is shown in his treatment of his subordinates. He had no favorites, no unworthy partialities. On one occasion he spoke highly of an officer and remarked that he ought to be promoted. Some surprise was expressed at this, and it was said that that particular officer had sometimes spoken disparagingly of him. "I cannot help that," said the general; "he is a good soldier, and would be useful in a higher position." As he judged of the work of others, so he judged of his own. A victory gave him pleasure only as it contributed to the end he had in view, an honorable peace and the happiness of his country. It was for this cause that even his greatest victories produced in him no exaltation of spirits: he saw the end yet far off. He even thought more of what might have been done than of what was actually accomplished. In the same way a reverse gave him

OPPOSITE: Robert E. Lee posed for Mathew Brady after the war at his home in Richmond. He is seated between his son, George Washington Custis Lee, and his adjutant general of four years, Colonel Walter H. Taylor.

pain, not as a private but as a public calamity. He was the ruling spirit of his army. His campaigns and battles were his own.

He frequently consulted others that his own judgment might be informed, not that he might lean on their judgment or advice. It was because he felt himself so completely the commander of his army that he sometimes assumed the responsibility of the failure of movements which a less strong and generous spirit would have made his subordinates bear.

There was no hesitation or vacillation about him. When he had once formed a plan the orders for its execution were positive, decisive, and final. The army which he so long commanded is a witness for him. He imbued it with his own spirit; it reflected his energy and devotion. Such an army, so responsive to orders, so rapid in movement, so sturdy and prompt in action, so often victorious, sometimes checked but never defeated, so patient in the endurance of hardships, yielding at last rather to the friction of battle and the pressure of hunger than to the power of the enemy, gives indication that its commander was gifted with that imperial quality . . . command.

As I recall the past, and the four years of the war come back and move in silent procession before me, I can easily forget that more than twenty years have passed away since I selected for General Lee the spot at Appomattox where his tent was pitched for the last time. His image stands out clearly before me, but it is unnecessary to describe his personal appearance. The majesty of his form will endure in marble and bronze, while his memory will pass down the ages as representing all that is greatest in military art, as well as what is truest, bravest, and noblest in human life – a soldier who never failed in duty, a man who feared and trusted God and served his generation.

"Vanquished,
He was yet a victor.
To honor virtue is to honor him;
To reverence wisdom is to do him
    reverence.
In life he was a model for all who live;
In death
He left a heritage to all.
One such example is worth more to earth
Than the stained triumphs of ten thousand
    Caesars."

Index

Alexandria, Va: 10, 65
Amelia Court-house, Va: 156
Anderson, Lt. Gen. Richard H., CSA: *6-7*, 6-7, 30, 47, 56, 81, 82, 86, 90, 91, 100, 102, 115, 120, 132, 139, 161
Antietam (see Sharpsburg)
Antietam Creek: 53, 55, 56, 58
Appomattox: 9, 161, 162, 164, 167, 179, 188
Arlington, Va: *11*, 12, 12, 14, *184*, 184
Arlington National Cemetery: 12, 184
Armistead, Brig. Gen. Lewis, CSA: 116, *117*
Army of Northern Virginia: 6-7, 7, 15, 18, 21, 24, 28, 49, 72, 78, 84, 94, 117, 122, 124, 128, 154, 156, 164, 167, 168, 169, 170
Army of the Potomac: *20*, 28, 29, 30, 32, *36*, 36, 49, 52, 61, 67, 68, 72, 75, 77, 78-79, 81, 93, 96, 102, 107, 118, 122, 128, 130, *130*, 149, 179
Averell, Maj. Gen. William W., USA: 80, 81

Baltimore, Md: 10, 13, 45
Banks, Maj. Gen. Nathaniel P. USA: 23, 30
Barksdale, Brig. Gen. William, CSA: 71, 81
Beauregard, Gen. Pierre G. T., CSA: *6-7*, 6-7, 147, *148*, 148, *176*, 176
Birney, Maj. Gen. David B., USA: 108
Blue Ridge Mountains: 106, 122
Boonsboro, Md: 47, 49, 50, 52-53
Brady, Mathew, B: 9, 51, 188
Bragg, Gen. Braxton, CSA: *6-7*, 6-7, *176*, 176
Bristoe Station, Va: 35, 36, 125
Brown, John: 14
Brown, Col. J. Thompson, CSA: 28, 71, 87, 93
Buckner, Lt. Gen. Simon Bolivar, CSA: *6-7*, 6-7, *176*, 176
Bull Run (see Manassas)
Bull Run (creek): 36, 38, 42, 125
Bull Run Mountain: 35, 36, 38
Burnside, Maj. Gen. Ambrose, USA: 29, 32, 40, 41, 43, 49, 49, 55, 56, 56, 58, 67, 69, 70, 71, 72, 74, 75, 77, 133, 139, 142, 143, 144, 145
Butler, Maj. Gen. Benjamin E., USA: *128*, 128, 145

Carter, Ann Hill (see Lee, Mrs. Henry)
Cashtown, Pa: 100, 101, 103
Cedar Mountain: 30, 31
Cemetery Hill (Gettysburg): 103, 105, *105*, 112, 113, *115*, 115, *116*, 116

Cemetery Hill (Petersburg): 144, 145
Cemetery Ridge: 102, 105, 106, 107, 108, 110, 111, 112, 174
Centreville, Va: 42, 43, 99
Chambersburg, Pa: 97, 99
Chancellorsville: 6-7, 80, *81*, 81, 82-83, *84*, 84-87, *87*, 88-91. 91, *92*, 92-93, 95, 96, 128, 132, 176: map; 84
Charleston, S.C: *15*, 15
Chickahominy River: 21, 22, 23, 24, 27, 96, 137, 138, 173
City Point, Va: 151, *152*, 152, *153*
Cobb, Maj. Gen. Howell, CSA: *50*, 50
Cobb, Brig. Gen. Thomas R. R., CSA: 72, 77
Cold Harbor, Va: 24, 25, 138-139, *139, 140*, 141, *141*, 142, 174
Confederate States of America: 15
Cooper, Gen. Samuel, CSA: *6-7*, 6-7
Culpepper Court-house, Va: 30, 31, 40, 66, 69, 98, 99, *122*, 122, 124, 125
Culp's Hill: 105, 111, 112
Custis, George Washington Parke: 11, 14
Custis, Mary Ann Randolph (see Lee, Mrs Robert)

Davis, Jefferson: 7, 15, *16*, 16, 19, 44, 98, 122, *176*, 176
Devil's Den: *120*, 120
Dinwiddie Court-house, Va: 151, 154
Drewry's Bluff: 16, *17*, 17

Early, Lt. Gen. Jubal A., CSA: *6-7*, 6-7, 35, 56, 91, 99, 101, 110, 119, 121, 129, 139, 149
Evans, Brig. Gen. N. G., CSA: 52, 56
Evergreen Cemetery: *105*, 105
Ewell, Lt. Gen. Richard, S., CSA: *6-7*, 6-7, 26, 27, 36, 38, *83*, 83, 97, 98, 99, 100, 101, 106, 107, 111, 112, 113, 117, 119, 121, 126, 129, 130, 131, 133, 161, *175*, 175

Falmouth, Va: 70, 71, 73, 95
Forrest, Gen. Nathan B., CSA: 6-7, 6-7
Franklin, Gen. William Buel, USA: 27, 42, 50, 55, 56, 71, 72, 74, 75
Frazier's Farm, Va: *27*, 27-28
Frederick, Md: 45, 46, 47, 49, 50, 100
Fredericksburg: 7, 21, 22, 23, 64, 67, 70, 71, 72-77, *77*, 81, 91, 92, 93, 94, 97, 98, 99, 129, 179; map: 72

Gaines's Mill, Va: 24, 25, 94
Gainesville, Va: 35, 37, 38
Gardner, Alexander: 51, 52, 56
Germanna Ford, Va: 126, 128, 130
Gettysburg: 7, 96, 97, 99, 100, *101*, 101-103, *103*, 104-120, 120,

122, *125*, 180; map: 100
Gettyburg Address: 127
Gordon, Maj. Gen. John B., CSA: *6-7*, 6-7, 133, 136, 139, 151, 164, 165
Gordonsville, Va: 30, 31, 129
Grant, Lt. Gen. Ulysses S., USA: 127, 128, 129, 130, 133, 136, *137*, 137, 138, 139, 141, 142, 143, 146, 147, 149, 151, 156, 161, 164, *165*, 165, *167*, 167, 169, 173, 174, 176, 177, 180, 182

Hagerstown, Md: 49, 51
Halleck, Maj. Gen. Henry W., USA: 48, *49*, 49, 66, 67, 99
Hampton, Lt. Gen. Wade, CSA: *6-7*, 6-7, 106
Hancock, Maj. Gen. Winfield S., USA: 113, 118, 128, 130, 133, 143, 144
Hanover Junction, Va: 23, 24, 137
Hardee, Lt. Gen. William G., CSA: *6-7*, 6-7
Harper's Ferry, W.V: *14*, 14, 45, 46, 47, 48, 49, 50, 51, 54, 55, 56, 94, 122
Heth, Maj. Gen. Henry, CSA: 90, 101, 102, 113, 115, 116, 119, 120, 131, 132, 154
Hill, Lt. Gen. Ambrose Powell, CSA: *6-7*, 6-7, 21, 24, 25, 25, 26, 27, 38, 43, 56, 58, 61, 72, 83, 88, 90, 97, 98, 99, 100, 101, 103, 106, 110, 113, 119, 120, 121, 126, 129, 130, 131, 133, 139, 154, *175*, 175, 177
Hill, Lt. Gen. Daniel Harvey, CSA: *6-7*, 6-7, 21, 24, 25, 26, 28, 30, 45, 49, 50, 51, 52, 54, 55, 56, 72
History of the Army of the Potomac (William Swinton): 61, 78, 81, 92, 117, 118, 130
Hollins, Gen. G. N., CSA: *176*, 176
Holmes, Maj. Gen. T., CSA: *6-7*, 6-7, 23, 24, 27
Hood, Maj. Gen. John Bell, CSA: *6-7*, 6-7, 26, 33, 37, 40, 52, 56, 107, 108, 109, 113, 115, 117, 120
Hooker, Maj. Gen. Joseph, USA: 55, 56, 58, 75, 78, 79, 81, 82, 83, 86-87, 88, 91, 92, 96, 97, 98, 99, 102, 128, 129, 174
Howard, Maj. Gen. Oliver Otis, USA: 79, 88, 101
Huger, Maj. Gen. Benjamin, CSA: 21, 24, 27, 28
Humphreys, Gen. Andrew A., USA: 108, 151
Hunt, Maj. Gen. Henry J., USA: *61*, 61, 71

Jackson, Lt. Gen. Thomas Jonathan "Stonewall", CSA: *2*, 4, *6-7*, 6-7, 15, 23, 24, 25, 26, 28, 29, 30, *30*, 31, 33, 35, 36, 37, 38, 40, 41, 42, 46, 47, 48, 49, 50, 51, 55, 61, 69, 70, 71, 72, 74, 82, *83*, 83, 84, *85*, 85, 87, *88*, 88, *90*, 90, 93, 94,

94, 95, 132, 173, *175*, *177*, 177
James River: 16, 20, 21, 27, 28, 128
Johnson, Maj. Gen. Edward, CSA: 111, 112, 119, 129, 136
Johnston, Gen. Albert Sidney, CSA: *6-7*, 6-7, 177
Johnston, Gen. Joseph E., CSA: *6-7*, 6-7, 15, *18*, 19, 20, 21, 161, *171*, 171, *176*, 176
Jones, Maj. Gen. David R., CSA: 56, 58, 1-6, 129

Law, Brig. Gen. Evander M., CSA: 107, 119
Lawton, Brig. Gen. Alexander R., CSA: 23, 26, 35, 56, 58
Ledlie, Brig. Gen. James H., USA: 145, 148
Lee, Agnes (daugher): *12*, 12
Lee, Cassius (cousin): 6
Lee, Maj. Gen. Fitzhugh, CSA: 80, 81, *82*, 82, 84, 87, 91, 154, 164, 165
Lee, Maj. Gen. George Washington Custis, CSA (son): 11, 12, *13*, 188, *189*
Lee, Henry "Light Horse Harry" (father): *10*, 10
Lee, Mrs Henry (Ann Carter Hill, mother): 10
Lee. Gen. Robert Edward, CSA: 1, 2, *4*, 4, *6-7*, 6-7, 8, *170, 172, 176*; background and birth 10; at West Point: 10, early career: 11-14, *14*, 170, 171; joins Confederate Army: 15; Seven Days: 16-29; 2nd Mansassas: 30-43, *37*; Sharpsburg: 44-62; field headquarters: 63-65; on McClellan: 66-67; Fredericksburg: 69-77; Chancellorsville: 78-95; last meeting with Jackson: *84*, 85, 86, 90; on Jackson's death:93; invasion of North: 96-9; Gettysburg: 99-120, 173, 174; headquarters: *104*, 104; retreat: 120-122; offers to resign: 122; against Meade: 124-127; The Wilderness: 130-133; Spottsylvania: 133-137; on Stuart's death: 136; Cold Harbor: 138, 141; Petersburg: 142-148, 152; appointed C-in-C Confederate Armies: 151; Five Forks: 151, 154; Appomattox: 156, 161, 164, 165, 166, *167*, 167, *169*, 169; military ability: 170-179; character: 180-188; death and funeral: 187, 188, *189*
Lee, Mrs. Robert E. (Mary Ann Randolph Custis): *11*, 11, 157
Lee, Lt. Gen. Stephen D., CSA: *6-7*, 6-7, 41, 42, 55
Lee, Maj. Gen. William Henry Fitzhugh (son), CSA: *82*, 82, 87
Lexington, Va: 6, 84, 170, 187
Lincoln, Abraham: 15, *60*, 60, *61*, 61, 66, 67, 75, 81, *126*, 127
Little Round Top: 108, 109
Long, Brig. Gen. Armistead L.,

CSA (author): *4*, 4, 7, 8, 16, 43, 44, 52, 62, 65, 71, 84, 86, 93, 97, 102, 103, 106, 113, 129, 132, 164, 165, 170, 182, 183, 188

Longstreet, Lt. Gen. James, CSA: *6-7*, 6-7, 21, 24, 25, 26, 27, 29, 30, 31, 33, 35, 36, 37, 40, 41, 42, 46, 51, 52, *52*, 53, 54, 55, 58, 66, 69, 70, 71, 72, 78, 82, 97, 98, 99, 100, 102, 103, 106, *107*, 107, 108, 109, 110, 111, 112, 113, 116, *116*, 117, 118, 119, 120, 121, 129, 131, 132, 133, 154, 165, *175*, 175

McClellan, Maj. Gen. George B., USA: 15, 21, 22, 23, 24, 25, 26, 27, 28, 29, 30, 40, 41, 42, 46, 48, 49, 50, 51, 52, 53, 54, 55, 56, 60, *61*, 61, 62, 66, 67, 93, 96, 173, 174

McDowell, Maj. Gen. Irwin, USA: 22, 23, 30, 37, 38, 173

McLaws, Maj. Gen. Lafayette, CSA: 47, 48, 50, 56, 81, 82, 86, 90, 91, 107, 108, 110, 113, 115, 117

McLean, Wilmer: 164, 167

Magruder, Maj. Gen. John Bankhead, CSA: 21, 24, 26, 27, 28, *175*, 175

Malvern Hill, Va: 17, 28, 29

Manassas: 96, 97, 99, 132, 176; First Manassas: 30, 40, 42; Second Manassas: 7, 30-43, *39, 40*; map: 38

Mansfield, Gen. Jospeph K. F., USA: 55, 56, 58

Marshall, Col. Charles, CSA: 16, 93, 167

Marye's Heights: *70*, 70, 71, 72, *73*, 73, 74, 76, 91

Maryland Heights: 47, 48, 49, 50

Massaponnax Church: 137

Massaponnax Creek: 69, 70, 71, 73, 81, 82

Meade, Maj. Gen. George Gordon, USA: *67*, 67, 74, 79, 99, *100*, 100, *102*, 102, 104, 105, 108, 109, 111, 117, 118, 120, 121, 122, 124, 125, 126, 127, 128, 130, 133, *137*, 137, 143, 145

Mechanicsville, Va: 22, 24

Meigs, Gen. Montgomery, USA: 12, 173

Mexican War: 12-13, 173, 179

Miles, Col. Dixon S., USA: 46, *47*, 47, 49, 50

Nast, Thomas: 167

North Anna River: 68, 130, 138

Orange Court-house, Va: 30, 31, 87, 129, 132

Peach OrchardL 107, 108, 110

Pemberton, Lt. Gen. John C., CSA: *6-7*, 6-7, 173, *175*, 175

Pender, Maj. Gen. W. Dorsey, CSA: 90, 101, 115, 116, 120

Pendleton, Brig. Gen. William N., CSA: 60, 71, 82, 90

Petersburg, Va: 6-7, 78, 141, *142*, 142, 143, 145, 149, 151, *152*, 154, 155, 156; map: 147

Pettigrew, Brig. Gen. Johnston, CSA: 115, 120

Pickett, Maj. Gen. George E., CSA: 113, 115, 116, 117, 118, 119, 120, 139, 154, 161

Pickett's Charge: *115*, 115-116, *116*, 117, 118, 119, 120, 121

Pleasanton, Maj. Gen. Alfred, USA: *86*, 87, 97

Pleasant, Lt. Col. Henry, USA: 143, 144

Polk, Lt. Gen. Leonidas, CSA: *6-7*, 6-7, *175*, 175

Pope, Gen. John, USA: 30, 31, 32, 33, 35, 36, 37, 38, 40, 41, 42, 43, 174

Porter. Gen. Fitz-John, USA: 24, 25, 26, 27, 55, *61*, 61

Potomac River: 44, 45, 46, 47, 49, 50, 55, 60, 61, 62, 66, 97, 99, 100, 106, 122

Price, Gen. Sterling, CSA: *175*, 175

Rapidan River: 30, 31, 69, 81, 122, 124, 126, 127, 128, 130

Rappahannock River: 21, 32, 33, 35, 36, 66, 67, 68, 69, 71, 72, 73, 75, 78, 81, *82*, 82, 91, 92, 93, 97, 98, 99, 125, 128, 179

Rappahannock Station, Va: 32, 35

Reynolds, Maj. Gen. John E., USA: 24, 79, *100*, 101, 118

Richmond, Va: 15, 16, 17, *18*, 18, 20, 21, 22, 26, 29, 30, 31, 67, 81, 93, 96, 128, 129, 133, 137, 138, 142, 149, 154, 156, *157*, 157, 158, 161, *180*, 181, *182*, 182

Ripley, Brig. Gen. Roswell, CSA: 23, 58

Rise and Fall of the Confederacy (Jefferson Davis): 19

Rodes, Maj. Gen. Robert E., CSA: 52, 53, 88, 90, 101, 119, 129, 139

Round Top: 105, 108, 109, 110, 112, 113, 120

Scott, Gen. Winfield, USA: 12, *13*, 13, 14, 15, 65, *172*, 173

Secession Hall: *15*, 15

Sedgwick, Maj. Gen. John, USA: *67*, 67, 79, 81, 82, 91, 92, 98, 107, 127, 128, 130, *133*, 133

Seven Days: 7, 16, 21-29; map: 17

Seven Pines: 6-7, 15, 18, 19, *20*, 20

Sharpsburg: 7, 44, 50, 51, 53, *55*, 55, *56*, 56-58, *58*, 59-60, *60*, 61, 66; map: 54

Shenandoah Valley: 15, 23, 49, 66, 69, 99, 122, 128, 173

Shepherdstown, W.V: 50, 55, 60, 62, 99

Sheridan, Lt. Gen. Philip H., USA: 136, 137, 143, 151, 154, 161

Sherman, Lt. Gen. William T., USA: 128

Sickles, Maj. Gen. Daniel E., USA: 79, 80, *86*, 86, 87, 107, 108, 109, 110, 111

Sigel, Maj. Gen. Franz, USA: 128, 141

Slocum, Maj. Gen. Henry E., USA: 28, 79

Smith, Gen. Edmund Kirby, CSA: *6-7*, 6-7

Smith, Gen. Gustavus W., CSA: 19, *21*

South Mountain: 49, 50, 97, 100, 104, 106, 122

Southern Historical Sociaty Papers: 84, 119, 131

Southern Review: 84, 86

Spottsylvania: *4*, 4, 133, 135, 136, 137

Stafford Heights: 73, 75, 96

Starke, Brig. Gen. William E., CSA: 56, 58

Stratford Hall: 10

Stoneman, Maj. Gen. George, USA: 81, 82, 87

Stuart, Maj. Gen. James Ewell Brown, CSA: *6-7*, 6-7, 14, 21, 23, 27, 30, 31, 32-33, 35, 36, 37, 40, 43, 49, 55, 62, 65, 66, 71, 74, 79, 82, 84, 86, 90, 91, 94, 98, 100, 103, 106, 127, 133, 136, 137, 175

Sumner, Gen. Edwin V., USA: 27, 42, 55, 56, 67, 69, 72

Susquehanna River: 97

Swinton, William: see *History of the Army of the Potomac*

Sykes, Mah. Gen. George, USA: 109

Talcott, Maj. T. M. Randolph, CSA: 16, 71, 86, 93, 165

Taylor, Lt. Gen. Richard, CSA: *6-7*, 6-7

Taylor, Col. Walter H., CSA: 16, 93, 111, 119, 131, 188, *189*

Thoroughfare Gap: 35, 36, 37, 38, 40

Traveller: 169, *170*, 170

Trimble, Maj. Gen. Isaac R., CSA: 33, 35, 56, 117

United States Ford: 70, 81, 91, 92

Venable, Col. Charles S., CSA: 16, 50, 52, 71, 93, 113, 131, 147, 164

Vicksburg, Ms: 173, 174

Vincent, Brig. Gen. Strong, USA: 109, 110

Virginia Military Institute: 93

Walker, Brig. Gn. John G., CSA: 47, 48, 56

Warren, Maj. Gen. Gouverneur, USA: 108-109, *109*, 127, 128, 130, 139, 144, 151

Warrenton, Va: 33, 35, 36

Warrenton Springs, Va: 32, 33, 36

Washington, D.C: 11, 12, 14, 22, 45, 81, 97, 99, 128, 173

Washington College: 12, *13*, *187*, 187

Waud, A. R: 37, 75, 81, 88, 139, 169, 179

Webb, Col. Alexander S., USA: *61*, 61

Weisiger, Brig. Gen. David A., CSA: *148*, 148

West Point: 10, 11, 12, 13, 14

Whiting, Maj. Gen. William Henry Chase, CSA: 21, 23, 26

Wilcox, Maj. Gen. Cadmus Marcellus, CSA: 37, 91, 115, 117, *131*, 131, 132

Wilderness, The: 81, 128, 129, *129*, 130, 131, 133, 136, 137, 174, *179*, 179; map: 127

Williamsport, Md: 46, 47, 49, 99, 122

Winchester, Va: 62, 65, 66, 94, 99, 122

Wolseley, Col. Garnet: *62*, 62

Yellow Tavern, Va: *136*, 136

York, Pa: 97, 99

Acknowledgments

The publisher would like to thank Ron Callow of Design 23, who designed this book, and Elizabeth Montgomery, who prepared its index.

All photographs are courtesy of the following sources:
The Bettmann Archive: 10(top left), 11(top left), 12(both), 13(both), 14(bottom), 15(both), 18(both), 29, 30(bottom left), 36, 43, 46, 50, 52, 53(bottom), 55, 59(top), 62, 63, 73(top), 74, 87, 95(top), 96, 98(top), 100, 101(top), 105, 110, 112, 116(both), 125, 139, 140(top), 144(bottom), 146, 151, 155(both), 157(bottom), 165, 166, 169(bottom), 171, 172-173, 174, 175(both), 176, 179, 180-181(both), 184-185(both), 186-187
Anne S. K. Brown Military Collection, Brown University Library: 2, 6-7, 31, 44, 57(bottom), 66, 69(bottom), 73(bottom), 81, 83(top), 85, 88, 89(top), 114(both), 115, 136
Chicago Historical Society: 76-77, 118, 119
DAR: 11(top right)
Rutherford B. Hayes Presidential Center: 131(top), 177(left)
Library of Congress: 1, 4(bottom), 8, 9(both), 10(bottom right), 11(bottom right), 14(top), 16, 20(both), 22, 23, 24, 25(both), 27(both), 28, 30(top right), 32, 37(both), 39(bottom), 41, 42, 45, 48(top), 49, 53(top), 54, 56, 57(top), 58, 60-61(both), 64, 65, 67, 68(bottom), 71, 75, 78, 79, 80(bottom), 82(both), 83(bottom), 87(bottom), 89(bottom), 90, 91, 93(both), 94, 95(bottom), 97, 98(bottom), 99, 102, 103, 104, 106, 107, 108, 109(top), 111, 113, 120, 121, 124, 126(both), 128, 129, 130, 131(bottom), 132, 133, 134-135, 137, 138, 140(bottom), 141, 142, 143, 144(top), 145, 148(both), 150(both), 153, 154, 156, 157(top), 160-161, 162-163, 167(both), 168, 169(top), 170, 177(right), 178, 182, 183, 189
The Museum of the Confederacy: 4(top), 70, 72, 122-123
National Archives: 26, 33, 34, 35, 40, 47(both), 68(top), 69(top), 77, 80(top), 86, 92, 109(bottom), 117, 152(both), 158-159, 164
Richard Natkiel: 101(bottom)
US Army Photograph: 21
US Army Military History Institute, Carlise, Pa: 19, 51
US Naval Historical Photograph: 59(bottom)